Contents

Cette publication est également offerte en français sous le titre suivant : *Stratégie de math
Rapport de la table ronde des experts en mathématiques, 2003.*

This publication is available on the Ministry of Education's website at http://www.edu.gov.on.ca.

D1401407

Early Math Strategy Expert Panel

Ruth Dawson (Co-chair)	Co-ordinator, Halton District School Board
Chris Suurtamm (Co-chair)	Assistant Professor, University of Ottawa Faculty of Education
Pat Barltrop	Teacher, Primary Grades, Toronto District School Board
Jane Bennett	Consultant, Halton District School Board
Ralph Connelly	Professor, Brock University Faculty of Education
Michelle Ferreira	Consultant, Durham District School Board
Johanne Gaudreault	Consultant, Conseil scolaire de district catholique du Centre-Est
Richard Gauthier	Director (retired), French-language Education Policy and Programs Branch, Ministry of Education
Heather Hutzul	Teacher, Kindergarten, York Catholic District School Board
Émilie Johnson	Consultant (retired), Conseil scolaire de district catholique Franco-Nord
Anna Jupp	Consultant, Toronto District School Board
Laurie Moher	Consultant, Kawartha Pine Ridge District School Board
Eric Muller	Professor, Brock University Department of Mathematics
Barry Onslow	Associate Professor, University of Western Ontario Faculty of Education
Francine Paquette	Teacher (retired), Kindergarten, Conseil scolaire de district catholique du Centre-Est
Estelle Rondeau	Teacher, Primary Grades, Conseil scolaire de district catholique Franco-Nord
Demetra Saldaris	Principal, Halton District School Board
Joanne Simmons	Consultant, Toronto District School Board
Lyn Vause	Consultant, Simcoe Muskoka Catholic District School Board
Nancy Vézina	Professeure adjointe, Faculté d'éducation Université d'Ottawa

Early Math Experts Addressing the Panel

Dr. Alex Lawson   Assistant Professor, Lakehead University
Faculty of Education

Craig Featherstone   Consultant, Halton District School Board

Dr. Lynne Outhred   Senior Lecturer, Macquarie University, Sydney, Australia.
Writer and researcher on the Count Me In Too project,
New South Wales, Australia

1 Introduction

Having identified the early grades of schooling as critical for a solid foundation in the basics of reading and mathematics, the Ontario government has been developing strategies aimed at improving achievement in reading and mathematics among children from Junior Kindergarten to Grade 3. In May 2002, the Ontario government announced that it would spend $25 million both to expand the year-old Early Reading Strategy and to create an Early Math Strategy that would help primary school students to improve their basic mathematics understanding and to begin to develop the mathematical skills needed in the twenty-first century.

Success in mathematics in the early grades is critical. Early mathematics understanding has a profound effect on mathematical proficiency in the later years. The *Early Years Report* by McCain and Mustard states: "We now know that a substantial base of mathematical understanding is set in the first few years" (1999, p. 9). A positive attitude towards mathematics, an understanding of key concepts, and mathematical skills must be developed in the early grades. Hence, the primary teacher plays an extremely influential and important role.

Research and experience have shown that the best way to raise student achievement is through a combination of doing intensive subject-focused work with teachers and setting improvement targets for student learning.

As part of the Ontario government's new strategy, a panel of experts in the learning and teaching of mathematics in the early grades was assembled to provide information and guidance on how best to support teachers and students. This panel was composed of practitioners and researchers from both the English-language and French-language educational systems as well as from various regions across Ontario. The practitioners and researchers on the panel assessed the current research-based knowledge of effective mathematics instruction and identified key components of an effective mathematics program and strategies for successful program implementation. There was much consensus on these key components in mathematics education.

Panel members compiled research and discussed best practice in the area of early mathematics education. Their meeting was an important opportunity to focus on early mathematics, and it provided an essential first step in focusing on mathematics in the early grades. This report summarizes the results of the panel meeting and the recommendations made by the panel.

The Ontario Curriculum, Grades 1–8 provides a framework for learning for students in all publicly funded English- and French-language elementary schools in Ontario. It outlines the knowledge and skills that students are expected to acquire by the end of each grade. Annual province-wide assessments of students' performance in reading, writing, and mathematics are conducted in Grades 3 and 6 as one measure of how well students achieve the expectations.

The current mathematics curriculum (*The Kindergarten Program, 1998; The Ontario Curriculum, Grades 1–8: Mathematics, 1997*) includes a broad range of knowledge and skills. The Grades 1–8 curriculum gives descriptions of the knowledge and skills required for each grade and links them with descriptions of achievement levels – different degrees of achievement of the curriculum expectations. This ensures consistency of expectations across the province and facilitates province-wide testing. Four levels of achievement are represented in the achievement chart, with level 3 considered as the provincial standard of achievement. The mathematics curriculum is divided into five strands: Number Sense and Numeration, Measurement, Geometry and Spatial Sense, Patterning and Algebra, and Data Management and Probability.

Yearly province-wide assessments are conducted by the Education Quality and Accountability Office (EQAO). Results are reported by school, by school board, and by the overall system. Over the five years from 1997–1998 to 2001–2002, system-wide results show that, while overall trends are generally moving in the right direction, large percentages of students are not achieving the provincial standard. Improving the mathematics education of all students is worthwhile.

Provincial Grade 3 EQAO Results – Mathematics
Percentage of Students Achieving at Levels 3 and 4 on Grade 3 EQAO Assessments

	1997–1998	1998–1999	1999–2000	2000–2001	2001–2002
English-language boards	43	56	57	61	58

The Early Math Strategy – like the Early Reading Strategy – is being undertaken by the Ministry of Education in response to this information. It has two complementary goals:

- *to reinforce the accountability of school boards and schools for improving student achievement through the setting of improvement targets, and*

- *to provide targeted supports to help elementary teachers, principals, and school boards work together to achieve consistently effective classroom teaching and assessment practices to support students' learning*

The supports being provided for the Early Math Strategy are founded on the belief, well attested in research, that teachers' knowledge of a subject and the skills that teachers can apply in the classroom have the most impact on students' learning. The Ministry of Education is supporting this strategy with many initiatives:

- *An Expert Panel was established to share research and best practice of teaching and learning mathematics in the early grades and to summarize its findings in this report.*

- *Learning resources in early math will be provided for students in the classroom.*

- *In-depth training of instructional leaders ("lead teachers") will be provided to ensure consistent implementation of the strategy across the province.*

- *Training materials will be provided for all elementary teachers to help them identify and use effective instructional practices and assessment strategies.*

- *Guides will be provided to parents on how they can help their children learn to do mathematics.*

- *Beginning in 2003–04, school boards will be required to establish targets for improvement for students taking Grade 3 mathematics.*

Target setting has been required since 2001 under the Early Reading Strategy and will be required as part of the Early Math Strategy, beginning in 2003–04, as noted. Boards and schools will set three-year targets for improvement, will develop plans to reach these targets, and will report on the plans to their communities and the ministry. Boards and schools will measure their success in reaching their targets and then adjust and refine their plans on the basis of information from school-based data and the EQAO Grade 3 mathematics assessment.

The early grades of schooling in mathematics are critical for the later success of all students. There are special issues in French-language schools that need to be taken into consideration, because in many regions such schools operate in a minority-language environment. The lack of an adequate foundation in French on the part of a number of children attending these schools has an impact on how mathematics is learned in the early grades and on what teaching strategies are used. The net improvement in Grade 6 EQAO results for French-language students seems to indicate that the acquiring of language skills by these students has a positive effect on student performance in mathematics. In later sections of this report, specifically those on the characteristics of the early math learner and on the framework for teaching, this issue will be more fully addressed.

3 The Teaching and Learning of Mathematics

Any discussion of the teaching and learning of mathematics in the early grades needs to consider several significant elements. In this report, these elements have been organized by considering two central components. These components are: the **characteristics of the early mathematics learner** and the **characteristics of an effective early grades mathematics program**. Within the discussion of an effective mathematics program, the following elements will be elaborated: a **sound learning environment** for early mathematics, a **framework for teaching**, the role of **assessment**, and approaches for ensuring **mathematics for all** students.

Characteristics of the Early Mathematics Learner

Many elements must be acknowledged about the early learner of mathematics. These include recognition of the developmental aspects of learning, the importance of building on prior mathematical understanding, and the essential fact that children learn mathematics primarily through **"... doing, talking, reflecting, discussing, observing, investigating, listening, and reasoning" (Copley, 2000, p. 29)**.

Developmental Aspects of Learning

Research across cultures and across socio-economic groups indicates that children go through stages of conceptual development that are identifiable (Clements, 1999). Several researchers have established continuums that delineate some of the growth points that children go through as they acquire various concepts in some areas of mathematics (Clarke & Clarke, 2002; Clements & Sarama, 2000; Griffin, Case, & Siegler, 1994). There is currently no agreed-upon continuum, because of the complexity and number of mathematical concepts. However, researchers do agree that children go through different stages of mathematical development. Also, there is considerable individual variation from child to child, and recognition of this variation is key to establishing the most effective learning environment. For the teaching and learning processes to be successful, it is important that the child's existing conceptual understanding of mathematics be recognized. Children need to encounter concepts in an appropriate manner, at an appropriate time, and with a developmentally appropriate approach.

> *Developmentally appropriate means challenging but attainable for most children of a given age range, flexible enough to respond to inevitable individual variation, and most important, consistent with children's ways of thinking and learning. (Clements, Sarama, & DiBiase, in press)*

Consequently, teachers must recognize the child's level of cognitive, linguistic, physical, and social-emotional development. The most effective learning takes place when these aspects of development are taken into consideration. This means that the child needs to be cognitively capable of taking on the mathematical task at hand; able to comprehend the language of instruction; have sufficient fine motor control to complete the task; and be emotionally mature enough for the demands of the task so that frustration does not hamper the learning situation (Sophian, in press).

French-language schools, in particular, have implemented two programs, called *Actualisation linguistique en français* and *Perfectionnement du français*, that address the need for some children to acquire the necessary language skills in French to pursue the curriculum expectations. Teachers play an important role at this critical language-development stage, in creating the classroom environment and using teaching strategies whereby children learn the language while being positive about learning mathematics.

Teachers should take into consideration the conceptual and developmental levels of their students in providing general guidelines for furthering children's development of concepts in mathematics. Teachers also need guidance in organizing the curriculum to allow for more time to be spent on important concepts in mathematics and to link such concepts with the developmental levels of their students.

Building on Children's Prior and Intuitive Knowledge of Mathematics

Children arrive at school with a variety of backgrounds and experiences and with more mathematical knowledge than was previously thought, regardless of different socio-economic situations (Ginsburg & Seo, in press). Children may not immediately communicate this understanding, but research on early stages of learning indicates that children begin the process of making sense of their world at a very young age, and this includes making mathematical sense (National Association for the Education of Young Children [NAEYC], 2002; Wright, Martland, & Stafford, 2000). **Young children have a natural inquisitiveness about mathematics, and teachers can build on this inquisitiveness to help students develop the positive attitudes that often occur when one understands and makes sense of a topic.** Research indicates that, when young children use mathematics to explore their world, their understanding can be quite complex and sophisticated (Ginsburg & Seo, in press). These initial understandings have powerful effects on how the child will assimilate and accommodate new knowledge (Bredekamp & Rosegrant, 1995).

Children also bring diverse cultural or linguistic contexts to their mathematics understanding. These linguistic, cultural, and community backgrounds, which result in distinctive approaches to learning and lead to a variety of prior knowledges in children, need to be recognized and valued. Research across cultures and across socio-economic groups indicates that all children go through various stages of conceptual development. Although the ages at which some children go through these stages is extremely variable, depending on their prior experiences, the actual sequence has some consistency (Bredekamp, Bailey, & Sadler, 2000; Clements, 1999; Ginsburg & Seo, 2000).

The mathematics that children bring to school should be valued and utilized in the classroom. Research points out that one of the difficulties in trying to improve the teaching of early mathematics is that teachers tend to underestimate the capabilities of young children when it comes to mathematics and may not have the knowledge to focus on important mathematical experiences (Sarama & DiBiase, in press; Sophian, in press). For instance, teachers may not realize that developing a solid understanding of the quantitative value of a number is as important as number identification and counting features.

Children need to see mathematics as sensible, and they do so when the mathematics they are learning in school connects with their intuitive sense of mathematics and with the understanding of mathematics that they bring with them to the classroom. Quite often students see school mathematics as different from the mathematics that they experience outside of school.

> Paul Cobb (as cited in Yackel, 2001) gives an example of such a situation. He conducted mathematical interviews with Grade 1 and 2 children and asked, "Do you have a way to figure out how much is 16 + 9?"

> Children used a range of methods including counting to solve the problem. Almost all of them were able to find the answer of 25. Later, students were given the same problem embedded in a typical page from a school text with a vertical format and instructions at the top for the standard North American addition algorithm with carrying.

This time many children attempted to use the standard school algorithm with carrying. While they had originally given correct answers some now had errors. The errors they made were ones that primary teachers would recognize, with some answers such as 15 or 115. When Cobb discussed the answer of 15 with one child and asked her whether both her original answer of 25 could be right as well as her latter answer of 15, she said that if you were counting cookies 25 would be right, but in school 15 would be the right answer. (Lawson, 2002)

Children's prior mathematical understanding needs to be recognized, to be developed, and to be connected with school mathematics.

Learning by Doing and Talking

The child invents mathematical knowledge from her or his actions on objects, so direct, concrete experiences with many objects at the child's developmental level are crucial to the formation of accurate concepts. (Maxim, 1989, p. 36)

Young children learn by doing, talking, and reflecting on their actions. They construct their own knowledge of mathematics using concrete materials and natural situations (Piaget, 1973). When students have opportunities to solve problems through doing, they develop multiple sensing pathways in the brain (McCain & Mustard, 1999). In fact, Ginsburg and Seo (in press) suggest that preschool children engage in a significant amount of mathematically related play. This mathematical play would include exploring patterns and shapes, comparing objects according to size, and developing a sense of number.

As a child matures, mathematically related play becomes problem solving, and children solve problems by creating models and using those models to communicate their understanding. Carpenter, Ansell, Franke, Fennema, & Weisbeck (1993) state that:

if we could help children to build upon and extend the intuitive modeling skills that they apply to basic problems as young children, we would have accomplished a great deal by way of developing problem-solving abilities in children in the primary grades. Furthermore, modeling provides a framework in which problem solving becomes a sense making activity. (p. 440)

Children arrive at school with intuitive mathematical understandings. A teacher needs to connect with and build on those understandings. This is done through the use of mathematical experiences that allow students to explore mathematics and to communicate their explorations in a meaningful dialogue with the teacher and their peers. As well, the activities that teachers provide need to be appropriate to the developmental stages of the students.

Characteristics of an Effective Early Grades Mathematics Program

An effective mathematics program has many elements that need to be well integrated. This integration of elements makes it difficult to isolate them for the purpose of discussion. However, a focus on the following elements – learning environment, framework for teaching, assessment, and mathematics for all students – seems to be a comprehensive way of discussing the complex issue of early mathematics education.

Overview of Learning Environment and Framework for Teaching

In order for the teaching of mathematics to be effective, there needs to be a sound learning environment or "backdrop" as well as an effective program of instruction and assessment. These two elements, however, must go hand in hand and are not necessarily clearly distinguishable. This **learning environment for mathematics** has many elements that will be discussed in detail in the next section. As shown in the graphic on page 12, these elements fit together much like the pieces of a puzzle, resulting in an environment that promotes student learning. The **framework for effective teaching** includes opportunities for guided mathematics, shared mathematics, and independent mathematics. This balanced framework will be discussed in detail later in the report.

The Learning Environment

An effective mathematics learning environment is an environment that:

- *promotes positive beliefs and attitudes towards mathematics;*

- *values prior knowledge;*

- *makes connections between that knowledge, the world of the child, and the strands and actions of mathematics;*

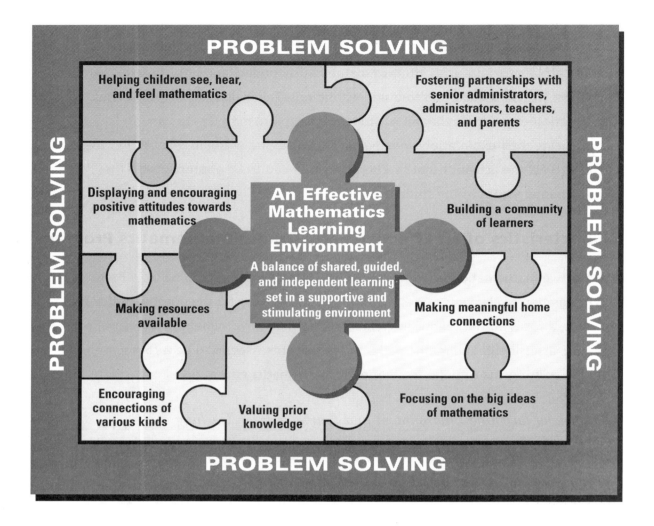

- *encourages the establishment of a community of mathematics learners;*

- *focuses on important mathematical concepts or big ideas;*

- *explores concepts through problem solving;*

- *includes a variety of learning resources;*

- *is supported by the strong roles of teacher, principal, and senior administrator;*

- *is supported by the home.*

The learning environment is a community of learners who feel that their knowledge and thoughts are valued, who feel safe to take risks in trying to solve problems, and who are comfortable talking about their understanding of mathematics.

Establishing Positive Beliefs and Attitudes About Mathematics

In a discussion of beliefs and attitudes about mathematics, it is important to consider the beliefs and attitudes of the child as well as the beliefs and attitudes of the teacher. Of course, other stakeholders in the learning process, such as the principal and parents, also influence children's attitudes towards mathematics. However, children's and teachers' feelings and attitudes about themselves and mathematics have a direct impact on teaching and learning.

> *Numerous studies provide data to indicate that there is a positive correlation between attitude and achievement in mathematics (Dossey, Mullis, Lindquist, & Chambers, 1998).*

Children's success with mathematics builds their positive attitudes and confidence. Mason, Burton, and Stacey (1982) and Lawler (1981) have documented the positive attitudes and responses that children have when they first make sense of a concept and build new connections. Children who build such connections increase their self-confidence in mathematics and develop positive attitudes towards the subject. Increased self-confidence and positive attitudes encourage children to make further explorations and additional discoveries.

Teachers are essential in influencing their students' attitudes towards mathematics, since those teachers who understand and enjoy mathematics generally provide positive experiences for their students. Teachers can facilitate attributes such as curiosity, creativity, enjoyment, flexibility, and perseverance. These characteristics are likely to lead to positive attitudes towards mathematics, and contribute to the students' continued enjoyment, confidence, and success in the subject. However, teachers who have developed a distaste for mathematics because it has eluded them or appeared abstract or confusing are likely to convey these negative feelings about mathematics to their students (Clements et al., in press).

Valuing Prior Knowledge and Making Connections

An effective learning environment values the prior knowledge that students bring to the classroom. The capabilities and knowledge of young children need to be recognized and valued. Teachers need to connect their teaching of mathematics with students' prior knowledge and understanding. Ginsburg and Baron (1993) found that:

> Young children come to school with a natural curiosity about quantitative events and some informal, yet powerful, problem-solving skills. These children have already constructed intuitive mathematical notions. We are challenged

to make use of the child's physical and social environment as motivating arenas for further quantitative reasoning and problem-solving. The research on children's cognition reveals the innate ability for all children to learn mathematics; it is up to us to guide their use of these informal skills to construct meaningful beginning notions of mathematics. (p. xii)

Meaningful mathematics instruction begins by engaging children's mathematical thinking, allowing children sufficient time to solve problems, and focusing on the use of incidental and integrated learning as well as programmed learning. However, teachers need strategies to help to assess prior mathematical knowledge and processes to guide further instruction. These assessment strategies include conferencing, interviewing, and observing children as they work and talk. Teachers also need to be aware of the curriculum that came before and comes after the current grade level.

> The most important connection for early mathematics development is between the intuitive, informal mathematics that students have learned through their own experiences and the mathematics they are learning in school. All other connections – between one mathematical concept and another, between different mathematics topics, between mathematics and other fields of knowledge, and between mathematics and everyday life – are supported by the link between the students' informal experiences and more formal mathematics. (National Council of Teachers of Mathematics [NCTM], 2000, p. 132)

Students do not enter school seeing mathematics as an isolated subject. It is an integral part of their world. From the perspective of young children, the world around them is not sectioned into different subjects such as mathematics or literacy (Basile, 1999). Because children's experiences are much more global in their essence, children can experience some mathematics concepts through problems and situations that people encounter in everyday life (Brandt, 1991; Lataille-Démoré, 1996). Children will learn to value mathematics through activities that help them build connections between mathematical concepts and between mathematics and other fields (House, 1990; Pallascio, 1990). These mathematical activities should have authentic mathematics content and depth, and must help the children move forward mathematically.

Mathematics for young children should be an integrated whole. Connections – between topics, between mathematics and other subjects, and between mathematics and everyday life – should permeate children's mathematical experiences. (Clements et al., in press)

In summary, effective mathematics instruction in the early grades makes connections with prior knowledge, between strands of mathematics, with the real world, and with other disciplines.

Building a Community of Mathematics Learners

Social interaction is one of the most important aspects of being a mathematician. A mathematics classroom, especially one that views students as young mathematicians, should include opportunities for social interaction (Kamii, 1985). A sense of mathematical community is fostered when teachers design classroom activities and groupings that promote intellectual sharing and value different ways of solving problems. Then, students can build on one another's knowledge through demonstrations, models, and questioning. When children have the freedom to talk, they can explore concepts, have their concepts challenged, and then make their own decisions about their learning. The community of the classroom must value these opportunities, and the teacher promotes community building by providing guidance about how such interactions can occur and by facilitating these interactions. As well, the environment for learning must allow students to feel safe and willing to take risks.

In a classroom community of mathematics learners, students will:

- *see, hear, and feel mathematics;*

- *learn mathematics through doing and talking about it;*

- *have enough time to solve problems and share with others;*

- *be active and enthusiastic about learning mathematics.*

Focusing on Important Mathematical Concepts or "Big Ideas"

> Much research indicates that children from diverse backgrounds can learn mathematics if it is organized into big coherent chunks and if children have opportunity and time to understand each domain deeply.... Successful countries select vital grade level topics and devote enough time so that students can gain initial understandings and mastery of those topics. They do not engage in repetitive review of those topics in the next year; they move on to new topics. (Fuson, in press)

Effective mathematics programs provide children with opportunities to have deep and sustained interaction with key mathematical ideas. A curriculum is more than a collection of activities: it must be coherent, focused on important mathematics, and well articulated across the grades. An effective program focuses on a number of key content areas rather than on trying to cover every topic or skill with equal weight (NCTM, 2000). Children's understanding is enhanced when they encounter concepts in depth and in a logical sequence. Such depth and coherence allow children to develop, construct, test, and reflect on their mathematical understandings. Consequently, teachers must have a good understanding of the key mathematical concepts and should themselves have explored these concepts in depth. Students must be helped to see that mathematics is an integrated whole, not a list of isolated bits and pieces (Van de Walle, 2001). **Teaching that uses big ideas or key concepts allows students to make connections instead of seeing mathematics as disconnected ideas.**

Teaching Through Problem Solving

Problem solving and reasoning are central to the learning of mathematics. Students learn mathematics as a result of exploring problems that provide rich challenges, relevance, and engagement. Problem solving helps to support core processes such as the use of representation, communication, and connection between and among mathematical ideas (Kilpatrick, Swafford, & Findell, 200l; NAEYC, 2002; National Research Council, 1989; NCTM, 2000). Also, children acquire their understanding of mathematics and develop problem-solving skills as a result of solving problems, rather than of being taught something directly (Hiebert et al.,1997). The teacher's role is to construct problems and present situations that provide a forum in which problem solving can occur. Many major international reports have confirmed that teachers need to use problem solving and reasoning as the focus of their instructional practice (Bowman, Donovan, & Burns, 2001; Bredekamp & Copple, 1997; Kilpatrick et al., 2001; NCTM, 2000; Pallascio, 1990).

Problem solving is more than the application of skills. Problem solving in a classroom generally begins with the teacher presenting the problem, students exploring and working on a solution to the problem, and then teacher and students consolidating and reflecting. In the first phase, when the teacher presents the problem, he or she may clarify the language or context, allow time for students to ask questions and seek more information, or ask students to restate the problem in their own words. During the exploring and solving phase, the teacher supports the students but avoids overassisting. Students solve problems by connecting with their prior knowledge and exploring and developing new knowledge and understanding. The teacher is available to respond to students' questions and uses the opportunity to observe and assess. During the consolidating/reflecting stage, the teacher facilitates the students' sharing of solutions and strategies. This is also an opportunity to stress communication, as students justify their solutions and explain their strategies. Students are guided to look at ways in which the problem connects with other problems or situations and to look at the specific mathematics concept that was explored.

Teachers need to recognize that problem-solving processes develop over time and can be significantly improved by effective teaching practices. Additionally, teachers can learn a great deal about students while they are solving problems because problem-solving opportunities provide teachers with insights into children's mathematical thinking. However, the problems need to be well constructed and challenging, so that they are not closed, with only one right answer that is easily determined. Students truly need to go through the process of solving a problem. This process may require that a student struggle and demonstrate persistence, but it will also bring understanding and confidence. Fennema et al. (1996) found that, when teachers used problem solving as the basis of all instruction, they became more knowledgeable about the myriad of ways in which children attempt to solve problems and students became more knowledgeable and confident in their problem-solving ability. This knowledge helped to inform and improve instruction.

The problem-solving process needs to be facilitated. This does not mean that particular strategies need to be taught or that students need to categorize types of problems and how they should be approached. Rather, it means that children's solutions to problems should be shared and discussed so that students can see a variety of approaches to solving a problem. There is not necessarily one right way to solve a problem; however, some strategies are more efficient than others.

> *Children do not need to be taught that a particular strategy goes with a particular type of problem. With opportunity and encouragement, children construct for themselves strategies that model the actions or relationships in a problem. (Carpenter & Fennema, 1999, p. 3)*

Of course, problems have to be meaningful to children. Research by Clements (2000, 2001) indicates that the younger the child, the more important it is to ensure that mathematical problem solving takes place in engaging contexts and within interesting projects. Problems need to be meaningful mathematically and contextually. Also, problem solving should not appear as an event but rather should be an integral process in a mathematics classroom.

Making Strong Home Connections

Parents, teachers, and children are all partners in the learning process. Countless studies over the years have clearly shown that, when parents are actively involved in their children's education, children do better at school (Epstein, 1991; Henderson, 1988; Henderson & Berla, 1994). For instance, children whose parents take an interest in their learning are more likely to talk about what they learn at school (Clark, 1983), develop positive attitudes towards mathematics (Glass, 1977; Hayes, Cunningham, & Robinson, 1977), and seek their parents' help.

Teachers and parents need to learn together and work together to support each child's educational journey. Home-school partnerships help parents connect with their children's learning. Teachers can discuss effective mathematics strategies with parents, who can then better understand how their children learn and can gain confidence when interacting with their children. Furthermore, parents who are helped to understand the content and pedagogy of today's mathematics teaching and learning are in a better position to assist their children's growth and development. The children will see a unified front between parents and teacher, rather than a struggle, with seemingly different methods of doing mathematics being communicated. **Opening channels of communication with the home sends the message to children that the mathematics at school is worthy and important.**

Teachers also benefit from strong home-school partnerships. They learn more about children's prior mathematical knowledge and experiences, and gain an increased understanding of children's cultural and linguistic backgrounds. Teachers who communicate with parents are able to explain to them, in a way that makes sense, the current mathematics curriculum and current teaching methods, and how these new strategies support their child's understanding of early mathematics concepts and skills.

Teachers and principals need to find ways to increase school-home partnerships and increase parental involvement in the education of their children. Some suggestions to strengthen the home-school partnership include:

- *determining the child's prior home mathematical experiences*

- *suggesting activities for parents, such as games that encourage success and practise mathematics*

- *helping parents understand the content and pedagogical processes of today's mathematics classroom (e.g., by sending home a brief description of the concepts and ideas involved in each new mathematics unit)*

- *providing ongoing communication regarding student progress*

- *preparing take-home mathematics kits that may include activities, literature, software, and manipulatives focused on a particular topic*

- *hosting school/family mathematics sessions, emphasizing mathematics activities that can be enjoyed by the whole family*

- *providing a calendar or a pamphlet outlining mathematics activities for families*

- *promoting the distribution and use of a parent guide on helping children learn mathematics*

- *involving libraries and bookstores by asking them to promote mathematical literature for young children*

Using Resources That Aid Understanding

Resources to support early grades learning of mathematics are essential. Resources take many forms. They include print resources for students, such as student books and mathematics-related literature, and print resources for teachers, such as professional development materials that provide support for the use of manipulatives, problem-solving activities, information about how students learn, and samples of effective teaching strategies. Resources also take the form of concrete materials or manipulatives that aid student learning in problem solving. In the early grades, music is also an important ingredient in an effective mathematics program, since children also learn through song. Furthermore, time is a valuable resource, and how a teacher structures the time spent on mathematics in a classroom is important. The organization or set-up of a classroom can also be seen as a resource, for it sets the stage for student learning.

Concrete Materials (Manipulatives)

> If we are to make mathematics experiential, we must present children with tactile tools with which they can learn, opportunities to interact with each other and the teacher, and diverse methods of arriving at the correct answer. (Murray, 2001, p. 28)

Concrete materials provide students with tactile experiences to help them model, describe, and explore mathematics. Manipulatives include such things as pattern blocks, base ten blocks, interlocking cubes, and many others that will subsequently be listed. Research suggests that manipulatives themselves do not magically carry mathematical understanding. Rather, they provide concrete ways for students to give meaning to new knowledge (Stein & Bovalino, 2001). Manipulatives also help the student to describe the mathematics and make the dialogue between students and between teacher and student more accessible. Children's mathematical thinking becomes more transparent when teachers observe children using manipulatives and listen to children's conversations.

As stated above, the use of manipulatives does not guarantee success (Baroody, 1989; Fennema, 1972). Guidelines need to be established on how manipulatives should be selected for classroom use, and teachers also need guidance on how to best use manipulatives effectively in the early mathematics program. Sowell (1989) suggests that attitudes towards mathematics are improved when students are instructed with concrete materials by teachers who are knowledgeable in their use. **Good lessons using manipulatives do not just happen; they need to be thoughtfully prepared.**

When selecting manipulatives, teachers should:

- *be certain that the manipulatives chosen support the selected mathematics concepts and big idea;*

- *have enough of the manipulative available so that all students can become active participants in the activity;*

- *provide initial opportunities for students to become familiar with the manipulative;*

- *communicate classroom procedures to students (e.g., refrain from using the manipulative when someone is sharing with the class; put manipulatives away in containers).*

When planning activities with manipulatives, teachers should:

- *use a manipulative in such a way that students then use it as a "thinking tool" enabling them to think about and reflect on new ideas;*

- *recognize that individual students may use the manipulative in different ways to explore mathematics;*

- *avoid activities that simply ask children to copy the actions of the teacher;*

- *allow students to use manipulatives to justify their solution as well as solve the problem;*

- *take time to become familiar with the manipulative chosen;*

- *choose manipulatives that will allow students to represent the mathematics in a meaningful way and to make connections from these representations;*

- *provide opportunities for students to explore the same concept with a variety of manipulatives.*

The following concrete materials should be part of an effective mathematics classroom.

Materials In a Primary Mathematics Classroom

Manipulative	Recommended for Every Classroom	Recommended for Every Grade/Division	Connections to Mathematical Concepts and Skills
Abacus		X	problem-solving/thinking skills, algebra/patterns, counting/skip-counting/one-to-one correspondence, relationships/connections, reasoning, place value, number concepts/operations, estimation
Attribute blocks	X		classification/sorting/making sets, symmetry, reasoning, patterns, data collection/management/graphing/interpretation, number concepts/operations, problem-solving/thinking skills
Balance and weights	X		measurement/scale, money, counting/skip-counting/one-to-one correspondence, reasoning, decimals, estimation, data collection/management/graphing/interpretation, reasoning, number concepts/number sense/number systems/whole numbers, classification/sorting/making sets, weight/mass
Base 10 materials	X		place value, money, measurement/scale, fractions, patterns, area, similarity/congruence, classification/sorting/making sets, number concepts/operations, perimeter, relationships/connections, problem-solving/thinking skills
Playing cards	X		counting, estimation, sorting, number concepts/operations, mental math, problem-solving/thinking skills
Connecting cubes (1 cm, 2 cm, 1.8 cm, and 2.5 cm)	X		number concepts/operations, counting/skip-counting/one-to-one correspondence, place value, classification/sorting/making sets, patterns, reasoning, symmetry, weight/mass, spatial visualization, probability/chance, area, perimeter, volume, quantity, transformational geometry, fractions, estimation, mental math, problem-solving/thinking skills, money, measurement/scale, relationships/connections
Connecting plastic shapes to build 2D shapes and 3D nets		X	classification/sorting/making sets, number concepts/operations, perimeter, counting/skip-counting, angles, reasoning, data collection/management/graphing/interpretation, one-to-one correspondence, similarity/congruence, area, problem-solving/thinking skills, spatial visualization, tessellations/tiling, fractions, transformational geometry, measurement/scale
Clocks	X Instructional clock	X Clocks for student use	time, fractions, measurement/scale, number concepts/operations, relationships/connections

Manipulative	Recommended for Every Classroom	Recommended for Every Grade/Division	Connections to Mathematical Concepts and Skills
Coloured tiles		X	patterns, estimation, counting/skip-counting/one-to-one correspondence, number concepts/operations, reasoning, place value, classification/sorting/making sets, fractions, problem-solving/thinking skills, probability/chance, measurement/scale, area, perimeter, odd/even numbers, data collection/management/graphing/interpretation, spatial visualization, similarity/congruence, relationships/connections
Coloured relational rods		X	classification/sorting/making sets, counting/skip-counting/one-to-one correspondence, number concepts/operations, similarity/congruence, fractions, symmetry, place value, patterns, odd/even numbers, reasoning, estimation, problem-solving/thinking skills, relationships/connections,
Dice/Numbered cubes	X		counting/skip-counting/one-to-one correspondence, number concepts/operations, mental math, fractions, probability/chance, decimals, problem-solving/thinking skills, classification/sorting/making sets, reasoning, data collection/management/graphing/interpretation
Geoboards (5 x 5, and 11 x 11) and geobands	X (Grades 2 and 3)	X (JK–Grade 1)	size, shape, counting, area, perimeter, symmetry, fractions, coordinate geometry, angles, estimation, similarity, congruence, rotations, reflections, translations, classification, sorting, polygons, spatial visualization, reasoning
Graduated beakers	X		measurement/scale, volume, estimation, fractions, mental math, problem-solving/thinking skills, number concepts/operations, counting/skip-counting/one-to-one correspondence, spatial visualization, data collection/management/graphing/interpretation, similarity/congruence, reasoning
Hundreds chart, hundreds board, hundreds carpet	X		place value, counting/skip-counting/one-to-one correspondence, estimation, patterns, number concepts/operations, fractions, probability/chance, odd/even numbers, spatial visualization, mental math, decimals, money, measurement/scale, volume, problem solving, relationships/connections, decimals, reasoning
Materials for counting and sorting	X		measurement/scale, patterns, estimation, relationships/connections, place value, counting/skip-counting/one-to-one correspondence, estimation, problem-solving/thinking skills, volume, fractions, number concepts/operations, classification/sorting/making sets, probability/chance, spatial visualization, odd/even numbers, data collection/management/graphing/interpretation, reasoning

Manipulative	Recommended for Every Classroom	Recommended for Every Grade/Division	Connections to Mathematical Concepts and Skills
Measuring spoons	X		measurement/scale, estimation, number concepts/operations, counting/skip-counting/one-to-one correspondence, data collection/management/graphing/interpretation
Measuring tapes		X	measurement/scale, estimation, number concepts/operations, counting/skip-counting/one-to-one correspondence, data collection/management/graphing/interpretation
Plastic transparent tools		X	symmetry, transformational geometry, angles, mental math, problem-solving/thinking skills, spatial visualization
Money	X – 1 set	X – multiple sets	money, counting/skip-counting/one-to-one correspondence, classification/sorting/making sets, fractions, probability/chance, problem-solving/thinking skills, estimation, mental math, place value, relationships/connections, data collection/management/graphing/interpretation, reasoning, measurement/scale, decimals, number concepts/operations
Number lines	X		place value, counting/skip-counting/one-to-one correspondence, estimation, patterns, number concepts/operations, fractions, probability/chance, odd/even numbers, spatial visualization, mental math, decimals, money, measurement/scale, problem solving, similarity/congruence
Pattern blocks	X		patterns, angles, counting/skip-counting/one-to-one correspondence, classification/sorting/making sets, tessellations/tiling, symmetry, area, perimeter, transformational geometry, problem-solving/thinking skills, reasoning, fractions, spatial visualization, data collection/management/graphing/interpretation, measurement/scale, number concepts/operations
Pentominoes		X	geometry, spatial visualization, problem-solving/thinking skills, patterns, reasoning, fractions, similarity/congruence, perimeter, angles, classification/sorting/making sets, symmetry, transformational geometry, number concepts/operations, area, tessellations/tiling, counting/skip-counting/one-to-one correspondence
Stackable blocks		X	number concepts/operations, counting/skip-counting/one-to-one correspondence, classification/sorting/making sets, patterns, symmetry, fractions, spatial visualization, perimeter, volume, area, problem-solving/thinking skills, estimation, transformational geometry, reasoning, money, probability/chance, measurement/scale

Manipulative	Recommended for Every Classroom	Recommended for Every Grade/Division	Connections to Mathematical Concepts and Skills
Stamps of various mathematical manipulatives (e.g., pattern blocks, tangrams, clocks, base 10)	X		
Tangrams		X	spatial visualization, problem-solving/thinking skills, patterns, reasoning, fractions, similarity/congruence, perimeter, angles, classification/sorting/making sets, symmetry, transformational geometry, number concepts/operations, area, symmetry, tessellations/tiling, counting/skip-counting/one-to-one correspondence
Thermometers		X	measurement/scale, estimation, number concepts/operations, counting/skip-counting/one-to-one correspondence, data collection/management/graphing/interpretation,
Two-coloured counters	X		measurement/scale, patterns, estimation, similarity/congruence, place value, counting/skip-counting/one-to-one correspondence, estimation, problem solving/thinking skills, fractions, number concepts/operations, classification/sorting/making sets, spatial visualization
3D solids	X		area, volume, classification/sorting/making sets, angles, reasoning, measurement/scale, symmetry, fractions, spatial visualization, perimeter, counting/skip-counting/one-to-one correspondence, geometry, area, problem-solving/thinking skills, number concepts/operations, weight/mass, relationships/connections, transformational geometry, tessellations/tiling
Trundle wheel		X	measurement/scale, estimation, number concepts/operations, counting/skip-counting/one-to-one correspondence, data collection/management/graphing/interpretation

Note: From *Supporting Leaders in Mathematics Education: A Source Book of Essential Information*, by the National Council of Supervisors of Mathematics, 2000. Adapted with permission.

Children's Literature

Making connections between mathematics and other curriculum areas is important in the early grades program. **Using children's literature as a starting point for a mathematics activity gives students a sense of how mathematics is connected with the world that they engage in when they read stories.**

Children's literature that supports an effective early mathematics program should:

- *connect with the Ontario curriculum* (The Kindergarten Program, 1998; The Ontario Curriculum, Grades 1–8: Mathematics, 1997);

- *provide authentic links between literature and mathematical ideas;*

- *include and promote the use of correct mathematical terminology;*

- *act as a prompt that leads to a mathematical investigation or question;*

- *offer varying levels of complexity;*

- *be based on fictional and non-fictional content;*

- *contain illustrations that display some of the mathematical concepts being addressed;*

- *include books for teachers to read aloud, as well as for independent student reading.*

Student Instructional Resources

A program requires a variety of resources to support student learning. The resources should be carefully chosen, and consideration should be given to the following factors.

Effective student instructional resources should:

- *connect with the Ontario curriculum* (The Kindergarten Program, 1998; The Ontario Curriculum, Grades 1–8: Mathematics, 1997);

- *provide background knowledge related to mathematics;*

- *emphasize the key concepts or big ideas of the relevant mathematics;*

- *provide lesson plans that are described in detail and include pre-teaching and follow-up suggestions;*

- *include activities that provide opportunities for students to demonstrate understanding, procedures, problem solving, and communication;*

- *contain single-strand and/or cross-strand activities;*

- *present open-ended problem-solving opportunities;*

- *allow multiple entry points for students;*

- *include suggestions for modifications and extensions;*

- *incorporate a range of instructional strategies;*

- *address multiple learning styles and intelligences;*

- *provide for a range of possible outcomes and/or student responses;*

- *include graphics and pictures that are recent and non-biased (e.g., in terms of gender, race) to illustrate processes;*

- *include tasks that are motivating and challenging;*

- *include a variety of assessment strategies by which students can demonstrate their learning.*

There continue to be a limited number of French-language learning resources in mathematics in Grades 1 to 3, as well as in Junior and Senior Kindergarten, both for print and for computerized material. Thus, there is a need for continued financial support to develop and to adapt and/or translate materials in the French language.

Calculators

Calculators should not replace paper-and-pencil tasks but should support them. When calculators are used appropriately in a mathematics program, their use does not interfere with students' mastery of basic skills and understanding. **To the contrary, their proper use (e.g., for generating patterns, problem solving) can enhance conceptual understanding, strategic competence, and attitudes towards mathematics (Groves & Stacey, 1998).**

Calculators that support an effective early mathematics program should:

- *have large, easy-to-use keys;*

- *have a one- or two-line display;*

- *display at least two decimals;*

- *provide stored operations with constants.*

Computer Software

The use of computer technology in a mathematics classroom allows teachers to provide students with visual representations to support dialogue about mathematics ideas. Good mathematics software should engage students as active learners, pose meaningful problems, and encourage collaboration with others (Ross, Hogaboam-Gray, McDougall, & Bruce, 2002).

Computer software to support an effective early mathematics program should:

- *connect with the Ontario curriculum* (The Kindergarten Program, 1998; The Ontario Curriculum, Grades 1–8: Mathematics, 1997);

- *promote mathematical communication;*

- *reinforce the use of problem-solving strategies;*

- *offer varying levels of difficulty, interaction, and complexity;*

- *be designed to meet the needs of early mathematics learners;*

- *be user-friendly;*

- *provide appropriate practice of isolated knowledge/skills.*

Classroom Organization

The organization of the classroom is an essential ingredient in the building of a classroom community of mathematics learners. To support an effective early mathematics program, a classroom should have:

- *a visible mathematics area in the room where core manipulatives are kept;*

- *manipulatives accessible to children throughout the day as needed, with routines established for their distribution and collection;*

- *manipulative storage bins or containers that are labelled for easy identification and clean-up;*

- *mathematical reference materials that are displayed around the room (e.g., calendar, number lines, hundreds charts);*

- *computers that are accessible to all children;*

- *areas for instructional groupings (whole group, small group, individuals).*

There should also be supplementary manipulatives available in the school's mathematical resource center. These manipulatives would not be required on a daily basis and could be shared among teachers in a primary division.

Time

The provision of sufficient blocks of time as well as the threading of mathematics throughout the day play vital roles in student learning. In Junior and Senior Kindergarten, there should be focused time (approximately 20 minutes) every day for mathematics; this may take the form of a guided or shared experience, or of students participating in a centre focused on mathematics. In addition to this time, students should be engaged in consolidating their mathematical learning in centres within the classroom (e.g., sand table centre, literacy centre, water table, and measuring centre). A minimum of one hour per day should be allocated to mathematics for Grades 1 to 3. Mathematics should also be integrated into other subject areas as appropriate. Mathematics concepts will also arise throughout the day, as lining up tallest to shortest is done or the number of minutes until recess is discussed, and teachers should make use of these teachable mathematical moments.

Recognizing the Important Role of the Teacher

> Effective mathematics teaching requires understanding what students
> need to learn and then challenging and supporting them to learn it well.
> (NCTM, 2000, p. 16)

Teachers have a profound impact on student learning. Having a positive impact is not an effortless undertaking. Effective teachers:

- *help students learn worthwhile and meaningful mathematical content;*

- *work effectively with a variety of students;*

- *provide meaningful mathematical activities;*

- *assess students' prior knowledge and build on it;*

- *value and organize resources and materials so that they are easily accessible to children when they are needed;*

- *encourage mathematics risk taking, ownership of learning, and communication between students;*

- *facilitate both cooperative strategies and individual practice, when appropriate;*

- *focus on building a sense of community, trust, personal sharing, and confidence;*

- *engage and value children's mathematical thinking.*

The Conference on Standards for Preschool and Kindergarten Mathematics Education suggests that:

> Teachers' most important role with respect to mathematics should be finding frequent opportunities to help children reflect on and extend the mathematics that arises in their everyday activities, conversations, and play, as well as structuring environments that support such activities. Teachers should be proactive as well in introducing mathematical concepts, methods, and vocabulary. (Clements et al., in press)

In order to facilitate students' mathematical understanding, teachers themselves need to develop a sound understanding of mathematics. Teachers need to know the mathematics that they teach as well as why they teach it. To a significant extent, good mathematics teaching rests in the teacher's ability to transform the mathematics content into forms that are accessible to students. "Although some teachers have important understandings of the content, they often do not know it in ways that help them hear students, select good tasks, or help all their students learn" (Ball, 2000, p. 243).

Some elementary teachers come to teaching with the experience of in-depth study of the subject area, while others develop knowledge through quality in-service and personal professional development. Before a teacher can develop powerful pedagogical tools, he or she must be familiar with the process of inquiry and the language of the subject and must also understand the relationships between information and the concepts that help organize that information in the discipline (National Research Council, 1998). Once teachers have an understanding of the content and pedagogy of mathematics, they then need to be able to use this knowledge in the practice of teaching. This means appraising and adapting materials, planning and instructing, hearing, interpreting, assessing, and designing appropriate ways to respond (Kilpatrick et al., 2001).

Needing the Supportive Role of Principals and School Boards

Principals and senior administration play an important role in supporting a positive learning environment for mathematics education. Principals and senior administrators need to foster a mathematics community in schools and school boards, where, for example, new teachers are mentored in mathematics instruction and all teachers are encouraged to share their best practices. Principals and senior administrators can enhance the home and school connections for mathematics. This includes collaborating with teachers, parents, school trustees, and the community in a dialogue about mathematics education. Principals and senior administrators may help secure the necessary resources for sound early mathematics programs. These resources include, but are not limited to, mathematics manipulatives, print materials, time, timetabling to encourage sharing among teachers of the same grade, and supporting and drawing on the expertise both within and outside the school community. Principals and senior administrators serve as instructional leaders and as role models of the lifelong learner, continuing to learn about effective mathematics education. **Principals and senior administrators should become familiar with the components of an effective mathematics program and should be able to recognize and encourage the use of those components in the classroom and in schools.**

Summary of the Learning Environment

Several factors come together to create an effective learning environment for early mathematics education. An effective learning environment should:

- *foster positive beliefs and attitudes about mathematics;*

- *value prior knowledge and make connections between important concepts in mathematics, the child's world, and other subjects;*

- *build a community of mathematics learners where mathematics is seen, heard, and felt;*

- *focus on important mathematical concepts or big ideas;*

- *encourage learning through problem solving;*

- *make strong links with the home and community;*

- *use resources that aid understanding;*

- *recognize and support the important role of the teacher;*

- *be supported by principals, senior administrators, and school boards.*

An effective teaching framework provides a balance of teaching strategies, a balance of student groupings, and a balance of types of activities. In this section, the importance of balance is discussed and an outline of a suggested teaching framework is provided to assist the teacher in maintaining that balance.

The Importance of Balance

Teachers have different styles and strategies for helping students learn mathematical ideas, and there is no one right way to teach mathematics (NCTM, 2000). Yet children benefit from a thoughtful combination of carefully planned sequences of activities and of integrated approaches that occur throughout the day (Clements et al., in press). These mathematical experiences vary from the incidental and informal to the systematic and planned (Kamii & Housman, 1999).

In an effective mathematics program, balance is the essential factor. In a discussion of balance, many things need to be considered. In particular, there needs to be a balance of the following:

- **skill development and problem solving**

  Carpenter, Fennema, Penelope, Chiang, and Loef (1989) found that, when instruction focused on problem solving, children not only became better problem solvers but also had better mastery of computations than did children whose instruction focused solely on drill and the practice of basic facts. Children need time to practise and consolidate skills, balanced with time to put those skills to use in a problem-solving context.

- **conceptual understanding and technical proficiency**

  A balanced program balances content and process and conceptual understanding and skill development. Research indicates that, if children memorize mathematical procedures without understanding, they find it difficult to go back later and build understanding (Resnick & Omanson, 1987; Wearne & Hiebert, 1988). Children may forget steps and confuse methods when they memorize without understanding. While developing fluency with basic facts is important, children need instructional strategies and approaches that allow them to develop meaningful and efficient methods for addition, subtraction, multiplication, and division.

- **teaching strategies**

  In an effective primary mathematics program, the teacher uses a balance of strategies, including play, exploration, investigation, direct instruction, and practice in a stimulating environment.

- **investigation and guided learning**

  Children need guided experiences to help them access mathematical knowledge. These guided experiences are most effective when they include active, concrete activities. Investigations provide students with opportunities to explore mathematical concepts using a variety of strategies.

- **individual activities and group activities**

  A variety of different groupings are effective. Students need time to communicate with their peers about mathematics and time to work independently.

- **activities to address different learning styles**

  Students learn in different ways; for instance, there are visual, auditory, and kinesthetic learners. It is important to use many different representations to address the needs of particular types of learners and to help to develop a broad range of learning styles in each child.

- **strands**

  A balanced program provides learning opportunities in all five strands. However, Number Sense and Numeration is a foundational strand for primary mathematics. Because number sense pervades the other strands of mathematics, it may be connected with mathematical activities in all strands and with mathematical teaching moments throughout the school day.

- **actions of mathematics or categories of the achievement chart**

  The categories of the achievement chart suggest that students should be engaged in developing knowledge and conceptual understanding, applying that knowledge, problem solving, and communicating. These categories of the achievement chart should be evident in instructional practices as well as in assessment.

- **assessment strategies**

  A variety of assessment strategies should be used so that all children have the opportunity to show what they know and can do in ways that best suit them.

  In *Adding It Up* (Kilpatrick et al., 2001) a mathematically proficient child is defined as one who has balanced development in the following areas:

  - conceptual understanding – comprehension of mathematical concepts, operations, and relations

  - procedural fluency – skill in carrying out procedures flexibly, accurately, efficiently, and appropriately

  - strategic competence – ability to formulate, represent, and solve mathematical problems

  - adaptive reasoning – capacity for logical thought, reflection, explanation, and justification

  - productive disposition – habitual inclination to see mathematics as sensible, useful, and worthwhile, coupled with a belief in diligence and one's own efficacy. (p. 116)

  The integrated and balanced development of all five strands of mathematical proficiency should guide the teaching and learning of school mathematics. Instruction should not be based on extreme positions that students learn, on the one hand, solely by internalizing what a teacher or book says or, on the other hand, solely by inventing mathematics on their own. (Kilpatrick et al., 2001, p. 11)

Components of a Balanced Program

In the building of a balanced program, three components are suggested. These include guided mathematics, shared mathematics, and independent mathematics. Although these components are listed and diagrammed in a specific order, that order does not reflect a sequence that must occur in a mathematics classroom. For instance, in the development of a concept, a teacher may use shared mathematics to allow students to explore the problem and discuss possible solutions; he or she may then use the technique of guided mathematics to help students with a new strategy that would be helpful in solving the problem at hand; the class may then engage in more shared mathematics; and then students could solidify the concept with an independent mathematical activity, such as using a manipulative to demonstrate their understanding of the concept. In each of these components, assessment and instruction are intrinsically linked. In other words, during the initial shared mathematics, the teacher may be listening and observing as a form of informal diagnostic assessment to see what prior knowledge the students bring to the situation. Demonstration with the manipulative may be viewed as an assessment activity that shows the teacher what the student has learned.

Fuson (in press) suggests that superior learning can take place using an effective method that has three phases. She suggests that, in the initial phase, teachers involve the students in introducing the concept through discussion and explanations. This phase also includes eliciting the student's prior knowledge about the concept. In the second phase, the student work is supported with help from the teacher and peers. As well, scaffolding (e.g., helping students break down a problem or providing steps and hints) would be added when deemed appropriate. Fuson suggests that this second phase helps students move from a dependent phase to an independent phase. The third phase is an independent phase in which students consolidate their understanding. Fuson's phases correlate with the components of guided mathematics, shared mathematics, and independent mathematics.

A description of each of the components of learning in a balanced mathematics program – shared mathematics, guided mathematics, and independent mathematics – follows. A discussion of linking instruction and assessment appears subsequently.

Shared Mathematics

Previous discussions have emphasized the importance of problem solving and communication in developing a mathematics community. This community can only come about through opportunities for students to share in mathematical activities. Shared problem-solving situations help students to develop problem-solving and reasoning skills. These opportunities allow students to make representations of mathematical ideas and connect such ideas with other concepts (Clements et al., in press; NCTM, 2000). These shared activities also afford teachers with opportunities to recognize the important concepts and strategies that are embedded in problem-solving activities. Naturally, play, exploration and investigation do not guarantee mathematical development, but they offer rich possibilities when teachers follow up by engaging children in reflecting on and representing the mathematical ideas that have emerged. Reflection occurs as teachers ask questions that provoke clarifications, extensions, and the development of new understandings (NCTM, 2000).

A summary of shared mathematics follows.

Shared Mathematics

Reasons for shared mathematics:

- Shared mathematics provides students with opportunities to acquire and use content knowledge and skills through problem solving, investigation, reasoning and proof, communication, connection, and reflection.

- Shared mathematics takes key concepts/big ideas from the curriculum that need to be addressed and considers how to incorporate them in a developmentally appropriate manner through problem solving or discussion.

- Students learn from one other. The teacher is not the only source of knowledge, and students need a variety of opportunities to construct their own mathematical understanding with others.

What shared mathematics looks like:

- Shared mathematics may occur between teacher and student, teacher and a group of students, student with other students.

- Reflection, discussion, and sharing occur at the end of the session to bring closure and clarification to the key mathematical ideas.

- Groupings could be pairs, small groups, or whole class.

Students could be:	The teacher could be:
• working in partners exploring a problem together;	• facilitating, observing, and asking key questions as students work;
• working at centres in small groups;	• promoting individual, small group, or whole group discussion;
• teaching other students;	• gathering assessment data to:
• using manipulatives;	– make decisions about where to go next with program planning;
• playing games;	– make modifications for individuals or groups of students;
• participating in a mathematics walk;	– provide extensions for individuals or groups of students.
• working on a puzzle;	
• working on computers;	
• singing songs to reinforce mathematical ideas;	
• exploring concepts, finding answers/solutions to problems, and generating or asking questions;	
• working together to learn a new concept/idea or skill;	
• talking, sharing – the classroom is productively noisy.	

Guided Mathematics

In guided mathematics, a teacher guides students through or models a mathematical skill or concept. This guidance affords students the opportunity to see an approach to solving a problem, to hear appropriate mathematical language, to view the teacher engaged in mathematical activity, or to participate in the activity as the teacher guides them through the concept.

A summary follows.

Guided Mathematics

Reasons for guided mathematics:

- Guided mathematics helps to clarify new knowledge or skill.

- Guided mathematics takes key concepts/big ideas in the curriculum and incorporates or presents them in a developmentally appropriate manner.

What guided mathematics looks like:

- Focus lessons are used.

- Instruction is sequential and planned by the teacher.

- Class instruction is well thought out yet flexible to capitalize on alternative ideas and strategies provided by students.

- The teacher works with the whole group or a small group, and at times with individual students.

- Reflection, discussion, and sharing are vital components to help bring closure and clarification of key mathematical ideas but need not occur at the end of class and may happen throughout.

- The teacher and students work with manipulatives, at a chart, standing in a group, at the overhead/blackboard, or sitting on the floor.

Students could be:	The teacher could be:
• responding to the teacher's questions and offering next steps; • guiding and modelling mathematical thinking or ideas for other students while the teacher provides support and guidance.	• activating the concept and connecting it with prior knowledge; • modelling mathematics language, problem solving, and thinking (think aloud); • leading the discussion and sharing; • setting up a learning experience so that students gain new knowledge or skills; • pointing out and highlighting students' different strategies while addressing the key concept/big idea or focus of the lesson; • acting as a guide or facilitator to ensure that strategies are appropriate, effective, and correct; • including good questions that are thought provoking and capture the essence of the mathematics.

Independent Mathematics

Independent mathematics helps students to consolidate and focus on their own understanding and think of ways to explain this understanding. Children are working on their own or in a group situation but on an individual task. They are able to ask for assistance and they know what assistance they need.

A summary follows.

Independent Mathematics

Reasons for independent mathematics:

- Children demonstrate their understanding, practise a skill, or consolidate learning in a developmentally appropriate manner through independent work.

- Students have time to grapple with a problem on their own.

- Students need time to consolidate ideas for and by themselves.

What independent mathematics looks like:

- Independent mathematics may occur at various times and not just at the end of the activity or lesson.

- Reflection, discussion, or sharing could occur to bring closure and clarification of the key mathematical concepts.

- Independent mathematics may include practising a mathematical skill, journal writing, explaining an idea to the teacher, playing an independent game, working alone on the computer, or using manipulatives to gain a better grasp of a key concept.

Students could be:	The teacher could be:
• communicating and demonstrating their learning;	• gathering assessment data to be used for diagnostic, formative, or summative purposes;
• at their desks, working on the carpet, at the board, using manipulatives, using clipboards, or working at computers;	• observing and recording anecdotal comments;
• working on their own but with the opportunity to ask a peer or teacher for clarification;	• walking around the room and interacting with students;
• completing a summative assessment task such as a performance task on their own;	• interviewing or conferencing with individual students.
• deciding which tools to use and where to find them.	

> ***Assessment should not merely be done to students, rather, it should also be done for students, to guide and enhance their learning.***
> ***(Van de Walle, 2001, p. 22)***

Assessment is the gathering of information or observable evidence of what a student can do. Evaluation involves the judging and interpreting of the assessment data and, if required, the assigning of a grade.

The purpose of assessment is to improve student learning. Teachers effect such improvement by coming to understand the mathematical thinking of the child and using such knowledge to inform and guide instruction (NCTM, 2000). Documenting the growth of such thinking is particularly challenging in the earliest years of schooling. A balance of assessment strategies that recognizes the importance of giving children the opportunity to talk about and concretely represent their understanding in many different ways is crucial to developing a complete picture of a child's mathematical understanding. This assessment should occur informally, on a daily basis, as teacher and students interact. Teachers should identify the quality of both the processes and products of a child's mathematical learning by making observations, using effective questioning, allowing for performance and problem-solving tasks, and collecting and appraising work samples that clearly illustrate student understanding in relation to concepts and skills. This type of formative assessment is the most valuable strategy for supporting children's learning, helping children to develop responsibility, and promoting children's autonomy as learners.

Linking Assessment and Instruction

> Research indicates that making assessment an integral part of classroom practice is associated with improved student learning. Black and William (1998) reviewed about 250 research studies and concluded that the learning of students, including low achievers, is generally enhanced in classrooms where teachers include attention to formative assessment in making judgments about teaching and learning. (NCTM, 2000, p. 1)

Quality instruction and appropriate assessment are not necessarily different activities and in fact should become nearly indistinguishable. In other words, teachers can assess as they provide opportunities for learning (Van de Walle, 2001). Effective assessment is an ongoing, integral part of the teaching-learning process and includes regular opportunities for children to demonstrate their learning (Connelly, McPhail, Onslow, & Sauer, 1999; Thouin, 1993).

Such effective assessment should:

- *inform and guide instruction and planning;*

- *be embedded directly in the daily instruction/activities of children so that feedback is immediate and effective rather than an end-of-week test that labels rather than fixes;*

- *reflect the mathematics that students should know and be able do (as related to the Ontario curriculum);*

- *be consistent with the content and processes in mathematics that are taught in the classroom;*

- *be ongoing.*

Principles of Assessment in Mathematics

Improvement of student learning in mathematics is the most important focus of sound assessment. Thus, assessment should always involve establishing clear criteria that are communicated to students and parents on a regular basis. Communication to students and parents throughout the assessment process is critical to successful learning. Information should be provided to parents to assist them in understanding the assessment process and how it helps identify the child's strengths and areas of need. As well, assessment in mathematics should include a variety of strategies and purposes.

The following criteria describe a sound assessment program. Assessment should:

- *be beneficial to children and their learning;*

- *identify children's mathematical strengths and particular needs;*

- *focus on the major conceptual and procedural understandings in the mathematics curriculum;*

- *reflect the mathematical competences and actions or processes of mathematics;*

- *use the categories in the achievement chart of the mathematics curriculum document for planning purposes;*

- *serve a variety of purposes: diagnostic, formative, and summative;*

- *be continual and promote growth in mathematics over time;*

- *provide clear criteria to make it easier for children to self-assess and set goals;*

- *use summative assessment and evaluation after sufficient time has been given for learning the relevant concepts and skills;*

- *include a variety of tools and strategies that assess both the processes and products of mathematics learning;*

- *help to establish what a student knows how to do and what areas need to be addressed and built upon;*

- *include a variety of assessment tools appropriate to the developmental level of the students;*

- *communicate clearly to parents and students what is assessed and how it is assessed;*

- *address the needs of all children, including those who need accommodations and modifications to the regular program.*

The Role of the Achievement Chart

A balanced unit would incorporate the categories of the achievement chart in both instruction and assessment. It is not expected that teachers would track these categories for grading purposes; rather, the categories provide a framework that gives students opportunities to demonstrate the understanding of concepts, the applying of procedures, problem solving, and communication.

Purposes of Assessment

A good mathematics program should also use assessment for different purposes: to determine prior knowledge; to identify developmental levels of mathematical understanding; to support day-to-day learning; and to set new goals. These purposes are addressed through diagnostic, formative, and summative assessment strategies.

Diagnostic Assessment: Assessing Prior Knowledge

The value of prior mathematical knowledge has already been explored. Teachers need to be able to determine the level of development and prior knowledge and understanding, so that appropriate teaching support can be initiated, the learning can be scaffolded appropriately, and assessment of progress can take place. How do teachers assess this prior knowledge? In the early grades, this diagnostic assessment does not need to be a formal assessment but could consist of a diagnostic interview, observation, pretests, questioning, and listening. In the early primary years (Junior and Senior Kindergarten, Grade 1) diagnostic assessment may be difficult to do because there is often no product to evaluate. However, through effective questioning and observation a teacher can determine where children are and help them access the next level of conceptual understanding (Sophian, in press).

Formative Assessment: Ongoing Assessment

Formative assessment provides immediate feedback to the learner and to the teacher to facilitate learning that is still in an alterable and formative stage. This feedback could be through observation, conferencing, interviews, daily tasks, journals, and possibly short quizzes, and can be used to help teachers decide when to provide additional experiences with a particular concept.

Summative Assessment: Determining What Has Been Learned

Summative assessment, which occurs at the end of a unit of study, assesses achievement and progress to date.

In the early grades, the main focus of assessment should be on informal diagnostic assessment of prior learning and formative assessment to support ongoing learning and to inform instruction.

Sound Assessment for Young Children

> Because young children's understanding can never be measured directly,
> a variety of tools and processes must be used so that reliable and valid
> inferences can be made from the evidence collected. (Copley, 1999, p. 183)

Young children show their understanding by doing, showing, and telling. Assessment strategies of watching, listening, and asking probing questions are needed to capture this doing, showing, and telling. Hence, observation is the most important focus in the primary classroom and should be an integral part of all other assessment strategies. Nevertheless, other assessment tools, similar to the tools used in other grades, should also be introduced. **Steffe and Cobb (1988) suggest that young children's ideas and methods of communicating those ideas can be overlooked unless teachers use a variety of assessment strategies.** However, these strategies need to be used in a developmentally appropriate way in JK–3 classrooms, with recognition that the way that assessment is used in Junior and Senior Kindergarten will be significantly different from how it is used in Grade 3.

In fact, especially in the early grades, there should not be an overemphasis upon paper-and-pencil tests. Assessment should be a positive, non-intrusive experience and should not make children feel less than they are. **Assessment should encourage students to show what they know and can do rather than focus on what they do not know or cannot do. An assessment that focuses on what students can do takes into account the developmental stage of the child.**

A holistic approach to assessment, taking into account the child's physical, social, emotional, linguistic, attitudinal, and cultural background, is most effective. In the early grades, daily informal observations and immediate feedback promote learning most effectively. Therefore, the major emphasis in the classroom should be on such ongoing formative observation and assessment.

A summary of research findings by the Education Quality and Accountability Office (EQAO) indicates that it is critical for teachers to base their judgement on several sources of information and a variety of assessment strategies (Berger, Giroux-Forgette, & Bercier-Larivière, 2002). Currently, teachers tend to record all assessment data and weight them equally when determining report card grades. Report card grades should not necessarily include all formative data collected but rather should reflect the stage of the student's achievement at the time of reporting.

Teachers need to use assessment strategies that provide as complete a description of the child's mathematical achievements and attitudes as possible. A description of such strategies follows.

- **Observations**

    Observation is probably the most important method for gaining assessment information about young students as they work and interact in the classroom. Teachers should focus their observation on specific skills, concepts, or characteristics, and should record their observations by using anecdotal notes or other appropriate recording devices.

    Observation is an essential skill of the early childhood teacher. Often thought of as only "looking" or "kid watching," observation also involves listening to interactions as they occur in natural settings. When teachers are observing children to assess their mathematical understanding, how the children carry out their work and the work they produce must be observed. (Copley, 1999, p. 186)

- **Interviews**

  Interviews are an effective tool for gathering information about young children's mathematical thinking, understanding, and skills. Interviews can be formal (Nantais, 1989) or informal, and are focused on a specific task or learning experience. Interviews include a planned series of questions, and these questions and responses give teachers information about attitudes, skills, concepts, and/or procedures. According to Stigler (1988):

  > Japanese teachers spend more time than do American teachers in encouraging their students to produce comprehensive verbal explanations of mathematical concepts and algorithms. This may contribute to Japanese children's success in mathematics. (p. 27)

- **Conferences/Conversations**

  A conference is useful for gathering information about a student's general progress and for suggesting some direction. A conference or conversation might occur in a one-to-one teaching situation or informally as a teacher walks around the room while students are engaged in solving problems. A student-led conference, in which students share their portfolios or other evidence of learning with parents or teachers, is an effective way of helping children articulate their own learning and establish new goals.

- **Portfolios and collections of work**

  A portfolio is a purposeful collection of samples of a child's work. These samples could include paper-and-pencil tasks, models, photographs of the student at work, drawings, journal entries, or other evidences of learning. This work is selected by the child and includes a reflective component that allows the child to connect with his or her own learning. Portfolios help to monitor growth over time (Jalbert, 1997; Stenmark, 1991). Portfolio assessment allows all learners to show what they know and can do. A variety of formats can be used, from a simple folder to a classroom portfolio treasure chest to document the class's mathematical growth.

- **Tasks and daily work**

  Daily classroom work provides an opportunity for immediate feedback and remediation. This instantaneous reflection by teachers allows them opportunities for making immediate accommodations to their programs.

- **Journals and logs**

  Journals allow students to share what they know about a mathematical concept. Mathematics journals can include written work, diagrams, drawings, stamps, stickers, charts, or other methods of representing mathematics. Journals also offer students the opportunity to describe how they feel about mathematics or about themselves as mathematics learners. It is important to consider the importance of oral sharing and the modelling of oral communication, which provides scaffolding for young children who are not always able to communicate all their ideas in written form. Journals for young children could be done orally with a tape recorder or as part of an interview.

- **Self-assessment**

  Students need opportunities for self-reflection and opportunities to think and talk about their learning.

- **Open-ended questions**

  Open-ended questions and their responses help teachers probe students' conceptual understanding and critical thinking. Such questions and responses allow for reasoning and the application of mathematical understanding and skills.

- **Performance tasks**

  Performance tasks help to assess what students can do. They are tasks that are generally authentic insofar as they simulate authentic mathematical challenges and problems. Such challenges and problems vary from purely mathematical tasks to tasks that are connected with real-life contexts.

- **Projects and investigations**

  Assignments or projects that are long-term assignments lend themselves to the development of problem solving and of higher-level thinking skills over time. If used in the primary grades, they should be highly scaffolded because of their complexity.

- **Test, quizzes, and short-answer questions**

  In the early grades, testing may cause anxiety, hindering students' natural instinct for learning. When tests and quizzes are used, they should have a balance of conceptual and procedural tasks, should allow for students to explain their answers, and should consider the developmental stage of the child. It must be emphasized that tests and quizzes are just a small part of the assessment program for the early grades.

> **Equity . . . means a classroom in which each child is included and affirmed as an individual and in which access to mathematical competencies valued by the culture is provided to all children . . . Equity means balancing the needs of various individuals and trying to organize socially to maximize the learning of all.**
> **(Fuson et al., 2000, p. 200)**

The belief that all children can learn significant mathematics is fundamental to early mathematics education (NCTM, 2000). The effective teacher will ensure that each child is given the opportunity to learn mathematics. To achieve this goal, educators face the challenge of meeting the needs of a diverse student population. This student population includes students with learning difficulties, behavioural challenges, and difficulties learning a new language, and students who are gifted in mathematics. One single instructional or assessment approach will not address the diverse needs of all students. Rather, a variety of teaching strategies need to be utilized. Effective intervention implies effective teaching, focused on meeting all students' learning needs, drawing on students' interest in mathematical ideas, challenging them, and fostering their confidence. All children are capable of experiencing success in learning when effective support is provided where it is most needed. Kilpatrick et al. (2001) suggest that "although existing research does not provide clear guidelines for teaching mathematics to children with severe learning difficulties, existing evidence and experience suggest that the same teaching and learning principles apply to all children, including special needs children" (p. 341). In other words, the descriptions of appropriate learning environments and effective instructional and assessment strategies also apply in the case of students with learning needs.

Knapp and associates (as cited in Fuson, in press) found that successful teachers in high-poverty classrooms were able to support conceptual understanding by focusing students on alternative solution methods and eliciting thinking and discussion about those methods rather than simply focusing on answers. Successful teachers also used multiple representations and real-life situations to facilitate understanding, and modelled ways to probe the meaning of mathematical problems or methods. All of these strategies are useful to all students. Generally, the same teaching and learning principles apply to all children, including special needs children.

However, children at risk for low performance in school mathematics should be provided with more support, as necessary. For some students, specific attention is needed, and this can involve a range of teaching approaches. For instance, a review of literature concerning the school success of diverse learners by Kameenui and Carnine, and by Geary (as cited in Fuson, in press) identifies crucial aspects of successful teaching and learning approaches for students with learning difficulties:

- *structuring learning around big ideas;*

- *teaching specific strategies when necessary;*

- *priming (e.g., eliciting or stimulating background knowledge);*

- *using mediated scaffolding such as peer tutoring, visual supports, cues for correct methods, feedback during thinking aloud;*

- *designing effective review (e.g., teaching specific strategies for learning basic facts focusing on number relationships – for example, facts with zero – over time with ample practice that is monitored and with immediate help for wrong answers);*

- *using visual rather than phonetic cues for students with verbal difficulties;*

- *allowing students with procedural deficits to use techniques that are less advanced but perhaps more conceptually based, for instance, "counting on" rather than a memorized strategy to calculate.*

As well, teachers of students who have English as a second language in English-language schools and French as a second language in French-language schools should:

- *assess the mathematical ability of second-language learners on the basis of cognitive ability and not on the basis of the student's proficiency in the language of instruction;*

- *work with a second-language support teacher, where available, to develop strategies to address the needs of second-language learners;*

- *provide children with opportunities to develop their own mathematical language, and gradually introduce appropriate terminology;*

- *assist in building connections and links in children's understanding;*

- *develop common understandings through direct instruction and exploration of ideas and meanings;*

- *encourage the home environment to foster and support the acquisition of the language of instruction in the school.*

Other strategies to assist students experiencing difficulty in mathematics include, but are not limited to:

General Organization and Instructional Strategies	Mathematics-Specific Strategies
Teachers could include:	Teachers could:
• enlarged materials;	• rewrite problems in simpler language;
• drawings and pictures;	• point out key words;
• calculators;	• minimize copying from boards by using handouts;
• manipulatives;	• have students do math on the board;
• adaptive devices: built-up pencils, highlighters, number line on desk, number stamps;	• have students repeat instructions;
• line indicators, sections on paper, graph paper or raised line paper;	• use boxes, circles, lines, and so forth to separate one problem from another;
• more white space for answers;	• turn lined paper to help make columns;
• less information on a page;	• develop mnemonics/cue cards (e.g., of the steps of various operations) that make sense to the child and tape them to the child's desk;
• fewer problems on a page;	• relate to real-life situations in word problems;
• students repeating instructions back to the teacher;	• use colour coding whenever possible;
• the use of diagrams, illustrations, pictures, multimedia, and concrete materials;	• use calculators;
• overhead projectors, flip charts, different-coloured pens/markers/chalk;	• reinforce math in other contexts;
• additional time to complete work.	• use games such as dominoes and dice.

In general, for effective intervention and remediation to occur, teachers should:

- *recognize that all children can learn mathematics;*

- *provide a supportive environment that fosters positive attitudes towards mathematics;*

- *build on the individual's prior knowledge;*

- *ensure the early identification of learning challenges in mathematics (e.g., through conferencing, school support teams) and provide intervention (e.g., small group, one-on-one, modified, alternative, or accommodated curriculum) to meet the needs of children with learning needs;*

- *use assessment strategies to determine individual student needs and develop appropriate action plans;*

- *work with a special education resource teacher and specialized board-level support, and use strategies that address the needs of exceptional students;*

- *use a wide range of remediation strategies;*

- *participate in professional development activities that address the special needs of children;*

- *involve families in supporting mathematics activities to further enhance positive attitudes towards mathematics.*

Principals and school boards support this work of teachers by:

- *providing extra support and resources for mathematics programs for schools with greater numbers of special needs students;*

- *increasing awareness in the community and building partnerships with organizations such as the Ontario Early Years Centres and learning disabilities associations to foster mathematics;*

- *providing professional development opportunities specific to early intervention and remediation in mathematics;*

- *providing or developing assessment tools to identify students who are at risk or who require enrichment in mathematics.*

> **Teachers who are ensuring learning for all children will incorporate a variety of strategies into their program and provide a supportive learning environment where all students are valued.**

Summary of an Effective Mathematics Program

An effective mathematics program should represent a balance and variety of teaching strategies, assessment strategies, student groupings, and types of activities. There should be opportunities to develop concepts through guided mathematics, shared mathematics, and independent mathematics. Through this variety and balance, the needs of all learners can be addressed and supported. An effective mathematics community and program requires the focused support of senior administration, principals, consultants and coordinators, and classroom teachers.

Developing and Sustaining Teacher Expertise

Characteristics of Effective Professional Development Models

Teacher knowledge of mathematics and skills in effective teaching are key to successful learning. Supporting teachers in developing this knowledge and these skills will in turn support students in their learning of mathematics. Good learning for teachers models, supports, and guides good learning for students.

Effective professional development involves active study over time of math content and pedagogy in ways that model effective learning and make direct connections with teachers' practice. Research on change indicates the importance of attending to individual teacher needs over time, providing learning opportunities tailored to those needs, and creating a climate of collegiality and experimentation and a capacity for continuous learning and support. These knowledge bases influence design decisions for effective professional development programs (Loucks-Horsley, Hewson, Love, & Stiles, 1998).

The purpose of the professional development of teachers is to improve student learning and understanding of mathematics. Successful professional development increases the teacher's confidence in and knowledge of mathematics and improves the teacher's understanding of how students learn mathematics. Such professional development should involve teachers in working on mathematics content and focusing on key concepts, exploring ways of determining a student's prior knowledge, and finding ways of providing connections to that knowledge in future learning. As well, teachers need to develop their understanding and experience of effective teaching strategies in mathematics. Many elementary teachers have mathematics anxiety, and this anxiety needs to be addressed in professional development activities so that a teacher may develop a positive attitude towards mathematics. The professional development should include the opportunity to link their new experiences with work in their own classrooms. This means trying out new strategies with their students and then having the opportunity to connect with colleagues to share their stories and to seek ways to continue their growth. Further, teacher growth needs to be supported by colleagues, principals, and the school board.

Professional development of teachers in French-language schools faces particular challenges: the relatively small numbers of teachers dispersed province-wide and the shortage of French-language resources make it difficult to organize training sessions in an efficient and cost-effective way, especially in those regions with a lesser French-language population concentration. There is a need to continue investing in information technology, since for teachers in French-language schools and schools in remote areas there is a greater dependency on video and Internet communications to build a network of learners and access resources. There are few French-language mathematics experts, particularly in early grades mathematics, who can provide the support and train teachers. These challenges need to be taken into account when designing effective professional development for French-language teachers.

The following is a summary of the components of an effective professional development program for all teachers of early grades mathematics.

Effective professional development must:

- **connect with student learning and the curriculum;**

  Professional development should provide experiences that will enable teachers to determine what students need to know, followed by processes that help students effectively construct this knowledge. In other words, professional development should make effective connections with curriculum. Teachers need to know how to choose and create resources in a manner consistent with the curriculum. They should also be encouraged to look critically at resources that synthesize mathematical concepts and bring out the big ideas. To a significant extent, good mathematics teaching rests in the teacher's ability to transform the mathematics content into forms that are accessible to students.

- **value the teacher as "learner" and help to foster a community of learners;**

  Professional learning for teachers should model the characteristics of good learning for students. These include: valuing a teacher's prior knowledge, encouraging teachers to build their own understanding of mathematics and mathematics education, learning through sharing, and allowing time to practise and reflect.

  In a collaborative learning culture, teachers should be supported to work together within their schools and boards to acquire a richer knowledge base and develop leadership skills. Professional development takes place both through structured and informal interaction and through group discussions among teachers. Frequently, however, these discussions need to be stimulated by an external resource person or consultant who has the knowledge of mathematics teaching and learning and who has experience in the elementary context to help to guide the discussion. Discussion among teachers who teach the same grade and share many experiences and issues can help teachers make sense of their experiences and feel less isolated, and can be helpful in generating new ideas and practices. In the case where a teacher is the only teacher of the grade or feels isolated in a small school or in a remote area, online discussion groups can serve as a community of learners.

- **connect with mathematics content and pedagogy;**

The ability to make mathematics accessible to students relies on a teacher's awareness of those aspects of mathematical content that are particularly relevant to its teachability. Lee Shulman has called this knowledge "pedagogical content knowledge" – that "special amalgam of content and pedagogy that is uniquely the province of teachers" (1987, p. 8). For any particular piece of content, pedagogical content knowledge includes knowledge of:

- what makes the topic easy or difficult to understand – including the preconceptions about the topic that students bring to their studies;
- those strategies most likely to be effective in recognizing students' understanding to eliminate their misconceptions;
- a variety of effective means of representing the ideas included in the topic – analogies, illustrations, examples, explanations, and demonstrations. (Shulman, 1986, pp. 9–10)

A central factor, then, for improving the teaching and learning of mathematics is increasing a teacher's pedagogical content knowledge. Teachers need to know the mathematics that they teach as well as why they teach it. And this knowledge should not just be a superficial understanding of a particular strategy. Teachers who are going to engage their students in mathematical problem solving need to fully understand the mathematics that may arise as students explore different types of solutions.

> *Teachers require opportunities to develop their understanding of both mathematics concepts and mathematics pedagogy.*

- **help teachers foster positive attitudes towards mathematics;**

Teachers' personal beliefs and professional histories play an important role in what teachers learn in professional development experiences (Darling-Hammond & Ball, 2000). The experiences should help to build positive beliefs about and attitudes towards mathematics – beliefs about learners and learning, teachers and teaching, the nature of mathematics, professional development, and the process of change (Loucks-Horsley et al., 1998). Professional development opportunities can be enhanced by providing teachers with occasions to examine their own teaching, discuss student learning, and share their reflective insights with colleagues. Growth also comes about for teachers when they engage in mathematical experiences themselves. Gadanidis, Hoogland, and Hill (2002) speak of rekindling the romance of mathematics in elementary teachers. They suggest that teachers, at some point in their early lives, enjoyed mathematics and perhaps had a bad experience with mathematics later in life that destroyed their confidence. Through exploring different types of problems and thinking of mathematics as a story, they suggest, teachers may again have success and feel positive about themselves as mathematicians, and this positive attitude is a necessary ingredient in helping their students to become positive mathematicians.

- **be ongoing and provide opportunities for communication, reflection, and refinement;**

  Professional development should be based on a cycle: developing awareness, building knowledge, translating into practice, practising teaching, and reflecting. Teachers need opportunities for analysis and reflection that include time, space, and encouragement. This analysis and reflection may take the form of talking with others, keeping a journal, engaging in action research (Darling-Hammond & Ball, 2000), or engaging in collaborative research (Bednarz, 2000).

- **recognize the value of a site-based component with a broader-based regional vision;**

  One of the main advantages of including site-based components in professional development models is that they can be tailored to suit the needs and objectives of the students, teachers, and administrators. However, the site-based model should also connect with a larger vision or initiative. Involving a lead teacher from every school in this initiative would provide that important link with the board and provincial focus. Such site-based models encourage school administrators, teacher leaders, and teachers to have some responsibility for professional development while connecting with a larger initiative that has a broader support base. This model increases accountability and empowerment, and provides a basis for sustaining growth beyond the short term. A system focused on mathematics promotes increased networking and sharing opportunities among families of schools or teachers of the same grade across a board, region, or province.

- **use a variety of models of professional development;**

  Effective professional development programs incorporate models such as:
  - coaching and mentoring
  - action research teams
  - study groups

- case studies

- lesson studies

- professional networks

- book clubs

The implementation of a variety of professional development delivery strategies will accommodate different levels of knowledge and learning styles.

- **provide a plan that will promote sustainability;**

Professional development should be long-term, with several short-term, realistic, manageable goals in mind. Long-term, sustained professional development facilitates change and improvement (Glickman, 2002). However, one of the main obstacles to professional development is a lack of time and of the resources that will facilitate effective collaboration and program development. Sound professional learning also needs to be continually supported by all stakeholders. These stakeholders include administrators at board and school levels, elementary mathematics consultants or coordinators, teacher mentors or facilitators, classroom teachers, and parents and students. Furthermore, professional development programs need to be continually evaluated and revised according to well-considered indicators.

To sustain ongoing professional development, lead teachers of mathematics require time to visit classrooms and meet with teachers. A reduced teaching load for lead teachers helps to facilitate the development of ongoing, sustained professional development. This initiative should also be supported by board-level elementary mathematics consultants or resource teachers, who are an integral part of support for early mathematics.

In other early mathematics initiatives, such as the Count Me In Too early mathematics initiative in Australia, lead teachers were given several release days to help to facilitate the development of other teachers, and this was considered essential to the success of the program (Outhred, 2002). Such an initiative also requires flexible timetabling and support from principals.

- **be supported by principals and senior administrators;**

    Principals are the key to creating the conditions for the continuous professional development of teachers and, thus, for classroom and school improvement (Fullan, 1992, p. 96).

Principals and other administrators need to be actively involved in the professional development process and make informed decisions about professional development at the board and school levels (Burch & Spillane, 2001; Payne & Wolfson, 2000). Informed principals use research and community and student profiles to work with staff to help to determine school improvement goals. Principals then connect professional development with whole-school improvement, teacher development, and classroom improvement (Newmann, King, & Youngs, 2000).

Principals and senior administrators also need professional training in what sound early mathematics experiences should look like, and should consistently improve their own understanding of good mathematics instruction. An effective professional development program includes professional development for principals and senior administrators in order to build awareness and support for early mathematics initiatives. As well, training of senior administrators at the board level ensures that board and school initiatives are correlated and consistent.

As school and board leaders, principals and senior administrators must provide support for effective mathematics teaching and learning by ensuring that appropriate resources are available, by creating and maintaining a collaborative school culture, and through the creative use of time.

Principals are also motivators and supporters of new initiatives. They need to be approachable and to acknowledge and encourage innovation and creativity in the classroom while recognizing that the steps to success are incremental and that change takes time. Effective principals are committed to the pursuit of "a continuous cycle of innovation, feedback and redesign in curriculum, instruction and assessment" (Newmann & Wehlange, 1995, p. 38) in the mathematics classroom and in the implementation of the new initiatives.

- **be supported by appropriate resources;**

  Teachers should have ready access to print, video, and computer materials to support their own growth and the growth of students. Such resources should be available to French-language mathematics teachers as well as English-language mathematics teachers.

  Effective professional development material should:

  – connect with the Ontario curriculum (*The Kindergarten Program, 1998; The Ontario Curriculum, Grades 1–8: Mathematics, 1997*);

  – provide background mathematical knowledge;

  – highlight the big ideas and key concepts of each activity;

  – offer suggestions on how to integrate strands;

- explain mathematical concepts clearly;

- demonstrate effective teaching strategies (e.g., cooperative groups, manipulatives use, quality questioning)

- include ways to intervene to support students at both ends of the spectrum;

- include ideas for ongoing assessment and evaluation.

In summary, sustained professional development, with strong links to curriculum and student learning, is effective. Such professional development helps teachers acquire knowledge, skills, attitudes, and beliefs about mathematics, helps develops their skills as reflective practitioners, and helps create a culture of teachers as learners.

Implementation and Research

Initiatives for improvement in teaching and learning require time, resources, the development of leaders, administrative support, and opportunities to monitor progress and adjust accordingly. The following section outlines roles for senior administrators, principals, and lead teachers. As well, suggestions are offered for helping to observe the implementation process and helping to determine its effectiveness.

Role of the Principal and Other Administrators

While there is no magic formula for school improvement, we have long known the importance of good principal leadership to positive school change.
(Carlson, Shobha, & Ramiriz, 1999, p. 17)

Effective leaders constantly work at helping individuals develop, continually work at enhancing relationships in the school and between the school and community, and maintain a focus on goal and program coherence. They focus on developing people, and building commitment to change and the conditions for growth while developing and acquiring resources (Day, Harris, Hadfield, Tolley, & Beresford, 2000; Leithwood, Jantzi, & Steinbeck, 1999; Sebring & Bryk, 2000).

Administrators are key to the successful implementation and sustainability of the Early Math Strategy. The following are descriptions of conditions that will support such an initiative:

- *Senior administrators facilitate the development of a system-wide commitment to early mathematics. Senior administrators communicate a shared vision across the board and assist principals in developing a shared vision of what their schools must accomplish in the area of mathematics instruction and student achievement.*

- ***Senior administrators align system focus. Senior administrators ensure that the alignment of initiatives is coherent at the provincial, system, school, and classroom levels.*** *Alignment and focus enhance communication, promote the sharing of resources, and foster a community of learners.*

- ***Senior administrators promote capacity from within.*** *Senior administrators create staffing practices that provide opportunities for the board and schools to hire elementary mathematics leaders. Elementary mathematics consultants and coordinators provide system leadership. Classroom teachers with expertise in early mathematics are provided with opportunities to share their practices both in their schools and across the board.*

- ***Senior administrators in the board have a process for supporting the principal and recognize that principals new to the role may need additional support and resources.*** *For example: The board may create solutions for allowing principals (especially those in one-administrator schools) to attend professional development sessions.*

- ***Administrators and principals are involved in the initiative through direct participation and support of teachers.*** *For example: Allowance for growth is critical; the encouragement of risk taking and a recognition of the incremental steps necessary for real change are needed. A system-wide focus on mathematics is shared with staff and reflected in decision making.*

- ***Senior administrators and principals provide support to teachers new to the profession who may need special/additional assistance.*** *Such assistance can be provided through mentoring, consultant support, additional professional development, and exposure to professional materials and journals.*

- ***Senior administrators and principals regularly share information regarding the progress of the Early Math Strategy with the staff and the community.*** *This can be done through staff and board meetings, bulletins, personal invitations, announcements, newsletters, communication binders, and so forth.*

- ***Senior administrators and principals are proactive in ensuring that necessary resources are purchased with monies earmarked for this purpose. These resources are outlined in section 3 of this report, "The Teaching and Learning of Mathematics".*** *Principals and senior administrators are encouraged to enhance these resources whenever possible through the use of external professionals, internal staff strengths, professional journals, the Internet, videos, trained volunteers from educational and community* programs, the effective placement of students in cooperative education, and board mathematics consultants and program services.

- **Senior administrators and principals support a program of feedback for this initiative.** Feedback informs implementation and allows for changes to be made along the way. Some suggestions for feedback during the implementation phase are made further in this report.

- **Senior administrators communicate regularly with board representatives and trustees on this initiative and its progress, and celebrate successes.** Increasing the awareness of sound mathematics educational practices in the early grades will enhance the entire educational community.

- More specifically, effective principals:

  - **attend and participate in the professional development sessions that arise from this initiative, and increase their knowledge of mathematics and its teaching;**
    For example: Increasing knowledge of mathematics and its teaching may be realized through taking summer courses, reading research and professional journals, visiting classrooms, and participating in resource reviews and selection.

  - **organize and oversee the professional development for the school as a whole;**
    Principals may use a variety of means to facilitate this process. For example: providing common preparation time and meetings, providing coverage for teachers, ensuring that teachers are able to attend professional development sessions, encouraging the development of blocks of time for mathematics instruction.

  - **provide an ongoing process for practice, sharing, collaboration, and reflection;**
    Principals are encouraged to celebrate successes and be supportive during setbacks.

  - **share information and materials with staff regarding professional development sessions;**
    This can be done through staff meetings, bulletins, personal invitations, announcements, newsletters, communication binders, and so forth.

  - **encourage the use of the mathematics resources available;**
    An inventory of mathematics resources may be made available for staff. In addition to classroom resources, a mathematics resource centre may be established and maintained, with an inventory available to all staff.

– *support community and home connections, and inform the school council of this initiative and its progress.*

As possible vehicles for meeting the objectives of this initiative, family math evenings, calendar math activities, meaningful home connections may be used to increase parental and community awareness. Mathematics resource inventories and needs may be shared with the council.

The Importance of the Lead Teacher

A lead teacher in each school, dedicated to improving early mathematics teaching and learning, will be essential to sharing information, helping to create a collaborative culture of teachers as learners, and improving student learning in mathematics.

Qualities of the Lead Teacher

The lead teacher should;

- *be enthusiastic about mathematics education*

- *see himself or herself as a life-long learner*

- *be a risk taker and be willing to try new things*

- *be a good communicator*

- *be respected by colleagues*

- *have a positive attitude, especially towards mathematics*

- *be willing to share ideas*

Role of the Lead Teacher

The role of the lead teacher may grow over time. Initially, the lead teacher needs to internalize and test out some of the new learning about mathematics education.

Therefore, initially, the role of the lead teacher will be to:

- *attend initial training sessions;*

- *gain confidence by implementing new mathematical strategies in his or her own classroom;*

- *reflect on his or her own practices – through a journal, interview, questionnaire;*

- *meet with other lead teachers from within the board or region.*

In subsequent years, the lead teacher will be able to:

- *attend professional development sessions;*

- *continue to implement new mathematical strategies in his or her own classroom;*

- *offer support to the primary team in the school;*

- *share resources and ideas with others on an ongoing basis;*

- *act as a mentor when appropriate;*

- *be a source of support for other teachers;*

- *be a team leader for the primary mathematics teachers in the school.*

Required Support for the Lead Teacher

A lead teacher will require the following:

- *professional development around sound mathematics concepts and good pedagogy*

- *resources for effective teaching and learning in the mathematics classroom, including manipulatives for students and resource materials to help the teacher provide sound classroom activities*

- *principal and board support to show that teachers' work and mathematics education are valued*

- *board-level support and resource people such as mathematics consultants or coordinators with expertise in elementary mathematics*

- *a network or communication link with other lead teachers and other professionals, for instance, the person who led the initial professional development session for the lead teachers*

- *suggestions on how to share with other lead teachers and maintain and support other teachers at the local level*

- *time for planning, reflection, and sharing*

It is important to research the implementation of the Early Math Strategy, as this will be the only means of evaluating change in a systematic way across the province. The research should be multifaceted and based on the improvement of teacher and student understanding of, and attitude towards, mathematics, and on the changes in classroom practice.

Both research projects and feedback activities should be included. For the purpose of this document, research projects are seen as well-structured projects in a local setting (e.g., case studies) or in a provincial setting (e.g., questionnaires). Feedback activities are seen as school-based projects that meet certain objectives but may vary from school to school in order to respond to local circumstances. These feedback activities will provide useful information to the stakeholders.

The research should aim to develop a full picture by including both quantitative and qualitative data and their analyses. It is also important that the research be multifaceted and based on the improvement of student understanding in mathematics and on the changes in classroom practice. Improvement in the student understanding of mathematics and in students' actions in mathematics can only be partially measured through EQAO scores. Other indicators must also be studied.

It is important to have feedback activities included as part of the monitoring of the implementation process. Feedback sessions will support and stimulate the many components of successful professional development models that are outlined in this report. Feedback will allow for adjustments to continually support and improve the effectiveness of the initiative.

Examples From Other Research Projects

In an early mathematics initiative in New Zealand, Count Me In Too (Thomas & Ward, 2001), the aim of the research on the initiative was the impact of the project on the participating facilitators, teachers, and students. The research was focused on the effectiveness of the facilitator training program and the impact of the initiative on the professional knowledge of the facilitators. The data were gathered through open-ended questionnaires at the completion of training and at the completion of the project. The research also looked at the effectiveness of professional development on teachers' professional knowledge. Through a questionnaire at the completion of the project, demographic and biographical data were gathered, and information on perceptions about program effectiveness was collected. Case studies were done of participating teachers in two schools.

These included semistructured interviews and concept mapping. A principal questionnaire studied principals' perceptions of program effectiveness. The effectiveness of the project on students was examined through two assessments, one at the completion of the professional development and another 15 weeks later.

The National Numeracy Strategy in England, part of the National Literacy and the National Numeracy Strategy (NLNS), was examined by school inspectors and also, through an external evaluation, by a group of researchers from the Ontario Institute for Studies in Education at the University of Toronto. This external evaluation was an extensive project that included data gathering over several years and included gathering national and regional data through monitoring documents, interviews, conferences, observations, and observation at meetings. At the local level, the data gathering included surveys, visits to schools to look at assessment data, lesson observations, and interviews with teachers, consultants, and numeracy managers (Earl, Fullan, Leithwood, & Watson, 2000; Earl, Levin, Leithwood, Fullan, & Watson, 2001).

Suggested Research and Feedback Models for the Early Math Strategies Initiative

It is assumed that the monitoring of school boards will be done by the Ministry of Education in terms of level of participation and use of resources. School boards will want to look at different schools to see how teachers and schools combine to affect teacher confidence and student learning. There should be an opportunity to see if differences in the types and amounts of professional development affect student learning.

The following suggestions outline possible research activities that could be coordinated on a provincial basis as well as suggestions for feedback activities for the local or regional levels.

Possible Research Activities – Provincial

Research on a province-wide basis should focus on the impact of the Early Math Strategy, and more specifically on changes in student learning in mathematics, and since student learning is so closely tied to the environment in which the learning takes place, should also consider changes in teachers' confidence in mathematics and their classroom mathematics teaching. Such research could include:

- *questionnaires reflecting schools' implementation: role of principal, types of professional development in mathematics, school resources, support for lead teacher (before and after)*

- questionnaires reflecting teachers' attitudes, beliefs, classroom practices, instructional and assessment activities

- questionnaires for lead teachers to reflect changes in lead teachers' attitudes, beliefs, classroom practices

- analysis of EQAO scores

- analysis of EQAO teacher surveys

- case studies of particular schools and classrooms to see how the implementation is played out

- case studies of lead teachers

Possible Feedback Activities – School and Regional

At the regional and school levels, feedback activities will help to support teachers and will provide information for making adjustments and improvements throughout the initiative. This feedback will allow for adjustments to be made throughout the process to better address the needs of students and teachers. Local feedback models will help to inform teachers' practice and will provide a clearer image of the school than can be obtained by examining EQAO scores alone. Some suggestions to allow for feedback at the local and regional levels include:

- online discussion groups for lead teachers within a defined geographical area

- specific suggestions for feedback to lead teachers as they work with other teachers

- classroom visits by the lead teacher

- concept maps of teachers' understanding of mathematics learning or of student understanding of a particular strand

- checklist of effective teaching strategies for teachers to help to determine where they are and to see where growth can occur

- teacher portfolios and journals

- teacher questionnaires

However, it is possible to combine provincial research and local feedback models. For instance, all lead teachers could be answering questionnaires that could be used as provincial data but could also be used by school boards to monitor progress of the initiative. The following feedback model is one suggestion that could provide information both at the local level and at the provincial level.

A Possible Feedback Model

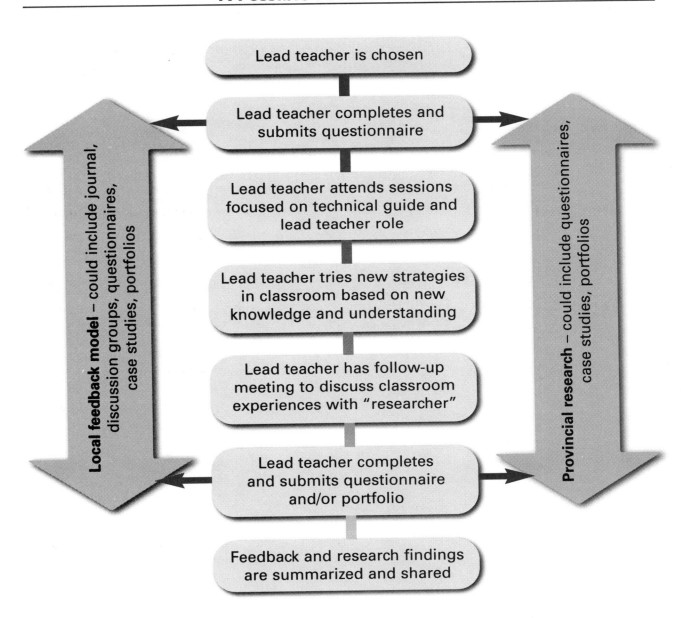

5 *Summary and Conclusions*

The following chart lists the components of an effective learning environment, an effective mathematics program, and an effective professional development program in early mathematics. A summary and discussion of these points follows the chart.

Early Mathematics Education Summary Chart

In an effective learning environment:

- a mathematical community is established and fostered throughout the year;
- teachers believe and show that mathematics learning can and should be enjoyed and understood;
- students and teachers display positive beliefs and attitudes about mathematics;
- students' prior knowledge is valued, and learning builds on children's mathematical ideas and strategies;
- school mathematics is connected with the child's world and other subjects;
- teachers emphasize and draw out key mathematical concepts during and/or towards the end of the lesson;
- big ideas of the mathematics curriculum are emphasized;
- students learn new mathematical concepts through exploring problems, explaining their mathematical thinking/ideas, and reflecting on their learning;
- teachers use a range of question types to probe and challenge children's thinking and reasoning;
- parents, teachers, and students work together to support mathematical learning;
- professional development opportunities for teachers explore mathematics concepts and pedagogy;
- principals and senior administrators support and foster a mathematics community within their school or school board.

An effective early mathematics program includes:

- a balance of guided, shared, and independent experiences;
- a variety of assessment strategies, including observation and/or listening to children, that are connected to the curriculum and reflect the developmental stages of the students;
- modifications to planning as a result of assessment;
- purposeful tasks that enable different possibilities, strategies, and products to emerge;
- blocks of time dedicated to mathematics;
- manipulatives that are visible and available, and utilized by students as they explore mathematical concepts;
- children's literature that is used as a springboard for mathematical dialogue and inquiry;
- sound print resources that are available to enhance student learning;
- calculators that are available to enhance, rather than replace, mathematical learning;
- computer software that engages students in meaningful problems.

Early Mathematics Education Summary Chart – *Continued*

Effective professional development in mathematics:

- values teachers' prior knowledge;

- builds mathematical understanding and confidence with mathematics;

- shares and promotes effective instructional and assessment strategies;

- connects with student learning, the curriculum, and classroom practice;

- allows time for practice, reflection, and meaningful dialogue and sharing among teachers;

- recognizes that growth takes time and requires ongoing sustained support;

- is supported and valued by the larger educational community: parents, principals, senior administrators, the school board, and the Ministry of Education.

Because the early grades of schooling are an important period of educational growth, positive, successful experiences with mathematics during this time are crucial. All students can learn significant mathematics if their learning environments encourage and support mathematics, and if the instructional and assessment strategies they encounter in the learning environment promote sound mathematics learning.

Developing a positive disposition towards mathematics and a belief in one's self-efficacy are critical components of a child's present learning and future achievement in mathematics. The learning environment must encourage a positive attitude, promote conjecturing and risk taking, encourage mathematical sense making, and help students make connections with their prior mathematical understanding and with the world around them. Developing and promoting such an environment is the work of the whole community. Specifically, parents, teachers, and children are important partners in the learning process. However, the support of others, such as principals, superintendents, elementary consultants, school boards, and the Ministry of Education, is also necessary to promote a positive mathematics community. By providing children with the necessary conditions for the successful learning of mathematics, our culture can nurture strong mathematics learners who approach mathematics with confidence and competence and continue to use and promote mathematics within today's society.

Good teaching and learning of mathematics recognizes that children come to school with a wealth of mathematical knowledge. Effective learning takes place when teachers plan mathematics programs that consider the child's level of cognitive, linguistic, physical, and social-emotional development. Children learn and understand mathematical concepts best when they are able to construct their own understandings through doing, talking, and reflecting, rather than watching. For this reason, children need the necessary resources, such as concrete materials, suitable technology, and problem-solving activities, to promote mathematical activity. As well, mathematical activity should be based on sound mathematics that focuses on the big ideas of mathematics. Mathematical activity based on sound mathematics is aided by teachers who have a sound understanding of the big ideas and are able to help students solidify this understanding through questioning, dialogue, and practice. Children should not be rushed through procedural tasks at the expense of developing conceptual understanding. **Students are helped to grasp fundamental mathematical concepts and their confidence in mathematics is built when they are engaged in meaningful problem solving and dialogue, and their new understandings and skills are reinforced.**

Since children show their understanding by doing, showing, and telling, sound assessment strategies should include observations, interviews, conversations, portfolios, and other techniques that involve components of dialogue and self-reflection. Observations and conversations are the primary means of assessing primary-level children and ensuring their growth. Simple observations by an effective teacher who is cognizant of the developmental states of children provide valuable documentation and evidence to support a child's growth in mathematical understanding.

Teachers make all the difference. Effective teachers have a large impact on student learning. Darling-Hammond and Ball (2000) suggest that:

> Teacher expertise – what teachers know and can do – affects all the core tasks of teaching. What teachers understand about content and students, for example, shapes how judiciously they select from texts and other materials and how effectively they present material in class. Teachers' skill in assessing their students' progress also depends on how deeply teachers know the content, and how well they understand and interpret student talk and written work. (p. 1)

An effective teacher needs mathematics knowledge, a comfort with and confidence in mathematics, an understanding of how children learn mathematics, and an understanding of effective instructional and assessment strategies.
A teacher also needs time to assimilate and use new ideas and information. Teachers need to have experiences that will help them construct their own understanding of good teaching and learning of mathematics. **Such professional development should model the features of good learning for students: prior knowledge is valued; new knowledge is developed; time is allowed for dialogue, practice, and reflection; and the support found within a community of learners is developed.**

Increasing teachers' pedagogical content knowledge through an effective professional development model that values growth over time can improve student learning and understanding. This professional development must be supported by all stakeholders, be ongoing, and be tailored to suit the needs of the students and teachers.

Children learn naturally when they are provided with engaging opportunities and challenges and are encouraged by their peers, parents, and teachers. The development of concepts and procedures during this period of cognitive growth is the foundation for future understanding and success in mathematics. For this reason, students need developmentally appropriate and balanced programs, a supportive community, and effective teachers. Developing and sustaining effective teachers requires the support of the entire educational community.

In conclusion, the Early Math Expert Panel recognizes the long-lasting impact that a solid early mathematical foundation will have on preparing students for future mathematics learning and experiences. The Expert Panel Report is an important first step in generating momentum across Ontario. **Change in beliefs, attitudes, and instructional practices will not, however, occur instantaneously: systemic change will require sustained effort, time, and resources, along with support from all stakeholders in the educational community.**

Glossary

achievement chart. A section in the curriculum policy documents. The achievement chart in the mathematics document identifies four categories of knowledge and skills in mathematics – problem solving, understanding of concepts, application of mathematical procedures, and communication of required knowledge. For each of these categories, four levels of achievement of the curriculum expectations are described.

achievement levels. The four different degrees of achievement of the provincial curriculum expectations. These are clearly described in the achievement chart in the curriculum policy document. Level 3, which is the "provincial standard", identifies the characteristics of student achievement that represent the expected level of achievement of the provincial expectations in that grade. Parents of students achieving at level 3 in a particular grade can be confident that their children will be prepared for work at the next grade.

assessment. The process of gathering information about students' knowledge and ability and of providing students with descriptive feedback to guide their improvement. Information may be gathered from a variety of sources (including observation and the recording and documentation of student work).

big ideas. In mathematics, key mathematical concepts. Helping students focus on these big ideas encourages students to make connections in mathematics.

conceptual development. The process by which the capacity to cognitively take on tasks and understand concepts is increased. This understanding of concepts is linked to the child's linguistic, physical, and socio-emotional development.

conceptual understanding. More than just knowing how to use a procedure, conceptual understanding is the ability to use knowledge flexibly, to apply what is learned in one setting appropriately to another.

developmental stages. Growth points in children's physical, intellectual, emotional, social, and moral development. Children proceed through developmental stages in their understanding of mathematics concepts.

evaluation. The process of judging and interpreting the information gathered through the assessment process and assigning a grade.

expectations (curriculum expectations). The knowledge and skills that students are expected to develop and demonstrate. The Ontario curriculum policy document for mathematics identifies expectations for each grade from Grade 1 to Grade 8.

instructional leader. An educator who stays abreast of current instructional thought and practices, and who understands current teaching models, strategies, and best practices. Such an educator is in a position to provide leadership to other teachers.

intervention. The provision of assistance to children who are at risk or have special needs that may affect their development. Intervention can be remedial or preventive.

learning styles. Different ways of learning. For instance, visual learners need to see visual representations of concepts. Auditory learners learn best through verbal instructions and discussions, by talking things through and listening to what others have to say Tactile/kinesthetic learners learn best through a hands-on approach, actively exploring the physical world around them.

mathematical concepts. Fundamental understandings about mathematics.

manipulatives (concrete materials). Objects that students handle and use in constructing their own understanding of mathematical concepts and skills and in illustrating that understanding. Some examples are base ten blocks, centicubes, construction kits, dice, games, geoboards, geometric solids, hundreds charts, measuring tapes, number lines, pattern blocks, spinners, and tiles.

model. A representation of an idea. This could be a physical model, such as a manipulative or a drawing.

modelling. Demonstrating to the learner how to do a task. Modelling often involves thinking aloud or talking about how to work through a task.

multiple intelligences. A way of classifying different human intellectual competencies, introduced by Howard Gardner (1993). These intelligences are:
*   linguistic intelligence
*   logical-mathematical intelligence
*   spatial intelligence
*   bodily-kinesthetic intelligence
*   musical intelligence
*   interpersonal intelligence

pedagogy. The study of teaching.

performance task. An assessment task in which students show what they know and can do. These tasks are generally authentic insofar as they simulate authentic challenges and problems. A performance task usually focuses on process as well as product.

problem solving. Engaging in a task for which the solution is not obvious or known in advance. To solve the problem, students must draw on their previous knowledge, try out different strategies, make connections, and reach conclusions. Learning by inquiry or investigation is very natural for young children.

procedural knowledge. In mathematics, knowledge of the appropriate procedure to select and cognizance of how to apply the procedure correctly.

professional development. Professional growth opportunities by means of which teachers can improve their learning and teaching. These can take a variety of forms, for example, action research, workshop attendance, journal writing, or taking courses.

remediation. The provision of special instructional assistance to students who are having difficulty attaining an established level of proficiency.

representation. The capturing of a mathematical concept or relationship in some form; also, the form in which a mathematical concept or relationship is captured. Students represent their thoughts about, and understanding of, mathematical ideas through oral and written language, physical gestures, drawings, and invented and conventional symbols.

scaffolding. A framework that helps students to tackle a problem, for example, the provision of hints or the breaking down of a problem into steps. The idea is that scaffolding is a temporary structure that can be removed gradually as students develop their problem-solving skills.

senior administrators. In school boards, the supervisory officers and directors of education who are responsible for the implementation of the Education Act, and of ministry and school-board policies regarding teaching and learning.

strand. A major area of knowledge and skills into which the curriculum for mathematics is organized. The five strands for mathematics in Grades 1–8 are: Number Sense and Numeration, Measurement, Geometry and Spatial Sense, Patterning and Algebra, and Data Management and Probability.

References

Ball, D.L. (2000). Bridging practices: Intertwining content and pedagogy in teaching and learning to teach. *Journal of Teacher Education, 51*(3), 241–247.

Baroody, A.J. (1989). Kindergartners' mental addition with single-digit combinations. *Journal for Research in Mathematics Education, 20*, 159–172.

Basile, C.G. (1999). The outdoors as a context for mathematics in the early years. In J.V. Copley (Ed.), *Mathematics in the early years* (pp. 156–161). Reston, VA: National Council of Teachers of Mathematics.

Bednarz, N. (2000). Formation continue des enseignants en mathématiques : Une nécessaire prise en compte du contexte. In P. Blouin et L. Gattuso (Eds.), *Didactique des mathématiques et formation des enseignants* (pp. 61–78). Mont-Royal, QC: Modulo Éditeur.

Berger, M.J., Giroux-Forgette, R., & Bercier-Larivière, M. (2002). *Learning and assessment of mathematics among Ontario francophone students in the early years*. Retrieved November 11, 2002, from Education Quality and Accountability Office website: http://www.eqao.com/eqao/home_page/pdf_e/02/02P028e.pdf

Black, P., & William, D. (1998, October). Inside the black box: Raising standards through classroom assessment. *Phi Delta Kappan*, 139–148.

Bowman, B.T., Donovan, M.S., & Burns, M.S. (Eds.). (2001). *Eager to learn: Educating our preschoolers*. Washington, DC: National Academy Press.

Brandt, R. (1991). On interdisciplinary curriculum: A conversation with Heidi Hayes Jacobs. *Educational Leadership, 49*(2), 24–26.

Bredekamp, S., Bailey, C.T., & Sadler, A. (2000, June–July). *The 1999 National Survey of Child Development Associates (CDAs)*. Paper presented at the Head Start National Research Conference, Washington, DC.

Bredekamp, S., & Copple, C. (Eds.). (1997). *Developmentally appropriate practice in early childhood programs* (Rev. ed.). Washington, DC: National Association for the Education of Young Children.

Bredekamp, S., & Rosegrant, T. (Eds.). (1995). *Reaching potentials: Transforming early childhood curriculum and assessment* (Vol. 2). Washington, DC: National Association for the Education of Young Children.

Burch, P., & Spillane, J.P. (2001). *Elementary school leadership strategies and subject matter: The cases of mathematics and literacy instruction*. Paper presented at the American Educational Research Association Meetings, Seattle, WA.

Carlson, K., Shobha, S.-S., & Ramiriz, D. (1999). *Leave no child behind: An examination of Chicago's most improved schools and the leadership strategies behind them*. Chicago Schools Academic Accountability Council.

Carpenter, T.P., Ansell, E., Franke, M.L., Fennema, E., & Weisbeck, L. (1993). Models of problem solving: A study of kindergarten children's problem-solving processes. *Journal for Research in Mathematics Education, 24*(5), 428–441.

Carpenter, T.P., & Fennema, E. (1999). *Children's mathematics: Cognitively guided instruction.* Portsmouth, NH: Heinemann.

Carpenter, T.P., Fennema, E.P., Penelope, L., Chiang, C.-P., & Loef, M. (1989). Using knowledge of children's mathematics thinking in classroom teaching: An experimental study. *American Educational Research Journal, 26*(4), 499–531.

Clark, R. (1983). *Family life and school achievement: Why poor black children succeed and fail.* Chicago: University of Chicago Press.

Clarke, D., & Clarke, B. (2002). *Stories from the classrooms of successful mathematics teachers: Painting a picture of effective practice.* Paper presented to the Early Numeracy Trainers, Melbourne, Australia.

Clements, D.H. (1999). Geometry and spatial thinking in young children. In J.V. Copley (Ed.), *Mathematics in the early years* (pp. 66–79). Reston, VA: National Council of Teachers of Mathematics, Washington, DC: National Association for the Education of Young Children.

Clements, D.H. (2000). *Geometric and spatial thinking in early childhood education.* Paper presented at the meeting of the National Council of Teachers of Mathematics, San Francisco.

Clements, D.H. (2001). Mathematics in the preschool. *Teaching Children Mathematics, 7*(5), 270–275.

Clements, D.H., & Sarama, J. (2000). Standards for preschoolers. *Teaching Children Mathematics, 7*(1), 38–41.

Clements, D.H., Sarama, J., & DiBiase, A.-M. (Eds.). (in press). *Engaging young children in mathematics: Findings of the 2000 National Conference on Standards for Preschool and Kindergarten Mathematics Education.* Mahwah, NJ: Lawrence Erlbaum.

Connelly, R., McPhail, S., Onslow, B., & Sauer, R. (Eds.). (1999). *Linking assessment and instruction: Primary years.* Ontario: Ontario Association of Mathematics Educators.

Copley, J.V. (1999). Assessing the mathematical understanding of the young child. In J.V. Copley (Ed.), *Mathematics in the early years.* Washington, DC: National Association for the Education of Young Children.

Copley, J.V. (2000). *The young child and mathematics.* Washington, DC: National Association for the Education of Young Children.

Darling-Hammond, L., & Ball, D.L. (2000). *Teaching for high standards: What policymakers need to know and be able to do.* (CPRE paper, No. JRE-04). Philadelphia: University of Pennsylvania, Consortium for Policy Research in Education.

Day, C., Harris, A., Hadfield, M., Tolley, H., & Beresford, J. (2000). *Leading schools in time of change.* Buckingham, England: Open University Press.

Dossey, J.A., Mullis, I.V.S., Lindquist, M.M., & Chambers, D.L. (1998). *The mathematics report card: Trends and achievement based on the 1986 national assessment.* Princeton, NJ: Educational Testing Service.

Earl, L., Fullan, M., Leithwood, K., & Watson, N. (with Jantzi, D., Levin, B., & Torrance, N.). (2000). *Watching and learning: OISE/UT evaluation of the implementation of the National Literacy and Numeracy Strategies.* Ontario: OISE/UT.

Earl, L., Levin, B., Leithwood, K., Fullan, M., & Watson, N. (with Torrance, N., Jantzi, D., & Mascall, B.). (2001). *Watching and learning 2: OISE/UT evaluation of the implementation of the National Literacy and Numeracy Strategies.* Ontario: OISE/UT.

Epstein, J.L. (1991). Effects on student achievement of teachers' practices. In S.B. Silver (Ed.), *Advances in reading/language research: Literacy through family, community, and school interaction* (Vol. 5, pp. 261–276). Greenwich, CT: JAI Press.

Fennema, E. (1972). Models and mathematics. *Arithmetic Teacher, 19*(8), 635–640.

Fennema, E., Carpenter, T.P., Franke, M.L, Levi, L., Jacobs, V.R., & Empson, S. (1996). A longitudinal study of learning to use children's thinking in mathematics instruction. *Journal for Research in Mathematics Education, 27*(4), 403–434.

Fullan, M.G. (1992). *Successful school improvement.* Toronto: OISE Press.

Fuson, K. (in press). Pre-K to grade 2 goals and standards: Achieving mastery for all. In D.H. Clements, J. Sarama, & A.-M. DiBiase (Eds.), *Engaging young children in mathematics: Findings of the 2000 National Conference on Standards for Preschool and Kindergarten Mathematics Education.* Mahwah, NJ: Lawrence Erlbaum.

Fuson, K.C., Carroll, W.M., & Drueck, J.V. (2000). Achievement results for second and third graders using the standards-based curriculum. *Journal for Research in Mathematics Education, 31,* 277–295.

Fuson, K.C., De La Cruz, Y., Smith, S., Lo Cicero, A., Hudson, K., Ron, P., & Steeby, R. (2000). Blending the best of the twentieth century to achieve a mathematics equity pedagogy in the twenty-first century. In J. Burke (Ed.), *Learning mathematics for a new century* (pp. 197–212). Reston, VA: National Council of Teachers of Mathematics.

Gadanidis, G., Hoogland, C., & Hill, B. (2002). *Mathematical romance: Elementary teachers' aesthetic online experiences.* Paper presented at the 26th Conference of the International Group for the Psychology of Mathematics Education, University of East Anglia.

Gardner, Howard. (1993). *Multiple intelligences: The theory in practice.* New York: Basic.

Ginsburg, H.P., & Baron, J. (1993). Cognition: Young children's construction of mathematics. In R.J. Jensen (Ed.), *Research ideas for the classroom, Early childhood mathematics* (p. xii). Reston, VA: National Council of Teachers of Mathematics.

Ginsburg, H.P., & Seo, K.H. (2000). Preschoolers' mathematical reading. *Teaching Children Mathematics, 4*(7), 226–229.

Ginsburg, H.P. and Seo, K.H. (in press). What is developmentally appropriate in early childhood mathematics? In D.H. Clements, J. Sarama, and A.-M. DiBiase (Eds.), *Engaging young children in mathematics: Findings of the 2000 National Conference on Standards for Preschool and Kindergarten Mathematics Education.* Mahwah, NJ: Lawrence Erlbaum.

Glass, J. (1977). An evaluation of a parental involvement program. Doctoral dissertation, Georgia State University. *Dissertation Abstracts International, 38.*

Glickman, C.D. (2002). *Leadership for learning: How to help teachers succeed.* Alexandria, VA: Association for Supervision and Curriculum Development.

Griffin, S.A., Case, R., & Siegler, R.S. (1994). Rightstart: Providing the central conceptual prerequisites for first formal learning of arithmetic to students at risk for school failure. In K. McGill (Ed.), *Classroom lessons: Integrating cognitive theory and classroom practice.* Boston: MIT Press.

Groves, S., & Stacey, K. (1998). Calculators in primary mathematics: Exploring number before teaching algorithms. In L.J. Morrow (Ed.), *The teaching and learning of algorithms in school mathematics. 1998 yearbook.* Reston, VA: National Council of Teachers of Mathematics.

Hayes, E.J., Cunningham, G.K., & Robinson, J.B. (1977). Counseling focus: Are parents necessary? *Elementary School Guidance and Counselling, 12*, 8–14.

Henderson, A.T. (1988). Parents are a school's best friends. *Phi Delta Kappan, 70*(2), 148–153.

Henderson, A.T., & Berla, N. (1994). *The family is critical to student achievement.* Washington, DC: National Committee for Citizens in Education.

Hiebert, J.C., & Carpenter, T.P. (1992). Learning and teaching with understanding. In D.A. Grouws (Ed.), *Handbook of research on mathematics teaching and learning* (pp. 65–97). New York: Macmillan.

Hiebert, J.C., Carpenter, T.P., Fennema, E., Fuson, K.C., Human, P.G., Murray, H.G., Ollivier, A.I., & Wearne, D. (1997). *Making sense: Teaching and learning mathematics with understanding.* Portsmouth, NH: Heinemann.

House, P.A. (1990). Mathematical connections: A long-overdue standard. *School Science and Mathematics, 90*, 517–527.

Jalbert, P. (1997). Le "portfolio scolaire" : une autre façon d'évaluer les apprentissages. *Vie pédagogique, 103*, 31–33.

Kamii, C.K. (1985). *Young children reinvent arithmetic: Implications of Piaget's theory.* New York: Teachers College Press.

Kamii, C.K., & Housman, L.B. (1999). *Young children reinvent arithmetic: Implications of Piaget's theory.* New York: Teachers College Press.

Kilpatrick, J., Swafford, J., & Findell, B. (2001). *Adding it up: Helping children learn mathematics.* Washington, DC: National Academy Press.

Lataille-Démoré, D. (1996). L'interdisciplinarité pédagogique. Paper presented at a symposium at the University of Moncton, NB.

Lawler, R.W. (1981). The progressive construction of mind. *Cognitive Science, 5*, 1–30.

Lawson, A. (2002, July). *Supporting effective primary mathematics instruction.* Paper presented at a meeting of the Early Math Strategy Expert Panel, Toronto.

Leithwood, K., Jantzi, D., & Steinbeck, R. (1999). *Changing leadership for changing times.* Buckingham, England: Open University Press.

Loucks-Horsley, S., Hewson, P., Love, H., & Stiles, K. (1998). *Designing professional development for teachers of science and mathematics.* Thousand Oaks, CA: Corwin Press.

Mason, J., Burton, L., & Stacey, K. (1982). *Thinking mathematically.* London: Addison-Wesley.

Maxim, G.W. (1989, December). Developing preschool mathematical concepts. *Arithmetic Teacher, 37*(4), 36–41.

McCain, M.N., & Mustard, J.F. (1999). *Reversing the real brain drain: Early years study, final report*. Toronto: Publications Ontario.

Murray, A. (2001, July). Ideas on manipulative math for young children. *Young Children, 56*(4), 28–29.

Nantais, N. (1989). *La mini-entrevue : un nouvel outil d'évaluation de la compréhension mathématique au primaire*. Montreal: Université de Montréal, Les publications de la Faculté des sciences de l'éducation.

National Association for the Education of Young Children. (2002). *Early childhood mathematics: Promoting good beginnings*. Statement of the National Association for the Education of Young Children (NAEYC) and the National Council of Teachers of Mathematics (NCTM). Washington, DC: Author.

National Council of Supervisors of Mathematics. (2000). *Supporting leaders in mathematics education: A source book of essential information*. Retrieved January 21, 2003, from http://www.mathforum.org/ncsm/NCSMPublications/2000/sourcebook2000.html

National Council of Teachers of Mathematics. (2000). *Principles and standards for school mathematics*. Reston, VA: Author.

National Research Council. (1989). *Everybody counts: A report to the nation on the future of mathematics education*. Washington, DC: National Academy Press.

National Research Council. (1998). *How people learn: Brain, mind, experience and school*. Washington, DC: National Academy Press.

Newmann, F., King, B., & Youngs, P. (2000, August). Professional development that addresses school capacity. *American Journal of Education, 108*, 259–299.

Newmann, F., & Wehlange, G. (1995). *Successful school restructuring*. Madison, WI: Center on Organization and Restructuring of Schools.

Ontario Ministry of Education and Training. (1997). *The Ontario Curriculum, Grades 1–8: Mathematics*. Toronto: Author.

Ontario Ministry of Education and Training. (1998). *The Kindergarten Program*. Toronto: Author.

Outhred, L. (2002, August). *Count Me In Too*. Paper presented at a meeting of the Early Math Strategy Expert Panel, Toronto.

Pallascio, R. (Ed.). (1990). *Mathématiquement vôtre : défis et perspectives pour l'enseignement des mathématiques*. Montreal: Agence D'ARC.

Payne, D., & Wolfson, T. (2000, October). Teacher professional development: The principal's critical role. *National Association of Secondary School Principals Bulletin, 84*(618), 13–21.

Piaget, J. (1973). *To understand is to invent: The future of education*. New York: Grossman.

Resnick, L.B., & Omanson, S.F. (1987). Learning to understand arithmetic. In R. Glaser (Ed.), *Advances in instructional psychology*, 3 (pp. 41–95). Hillsdale, NJ: Lawrence Erlbaum.

Ross, J., Hogaboam-Gray, A., McDougall, D., & Bruce, C. (2002). *The contribution of technology to mathematics education reform*. Paper presented at the American Educational Research Association Conference, New Orleans, LA.

Sarama, J., & DiBiase, A.-M. (in press). The professional development challenge in preschool mathematics. In D.H. Clements, J. Sarama, & A.-M. DiBiase (Eds.), *Engaging young children in mathematics: Findings of the 2000 National Conference on Standards for Preschool and Kindergarten Mathematics Education*. Mahwah, NJ: Lawrence Erlbaum.

Sebring, P., & Bryk, A. (2000, February). School leadership and the bottom line in Chicago. *Phi Delta Kappan, 81*(6), 440–443.

Shulman, L.S. (1986). Those who understand: Knowledge growth in teaching. *Educational Researcher, 15*(2), 4–14.

Shulman, L.S. (1987). Knowledge and teaching: Foundations of the new reform. *Harvard Educational Review, 57*(1), 1–22.

Sophian, C. (in press). A prospective developmental perspective on early mathematics instruction. In D.H. Clements, J. Sarama, & A-M. DiBiase (Eds.), *Engaging young children in mathematics: Findings of the 2000 National Conference on Standards for Preschool and Kindergarten Mathematics Education*. Mahwah, NJ: Lawrence Erlbaum.

Sowell, E.J. (1989, November). Effects of manipulative materials in mathematics instruction. *Journal for Research in Mathematics Education, 20*(5), 498–505.

Steffe, L.P., & Cobb, P. (1988). *Construction of arithmetical meanings and strategies.* New York: Springer-Verlag.

Stein, J.K., & Bovalino, J. (2001). Manipulatives: One piece of the puzzle. *Mathematics Teaching in the Middle School, 6*(6), 356–359.

Stenmark, J. (Ed.). (1991). *Mathematics assessment: Myths, models, good questions, and practical suggestions.* Reston, VA: National Council of Teachers of Mathematics.

Stigler, J.W. (1988, October). Research into practice: The use of verbal explanation in Japanese and American classrooms. *Arithmetic Teacher*, 27–29.

Thomas, G., & Ward, J. (2001). *Exploring issues in mathematics education: An evaluation of the Early Numeracy Project 2001.* New Zealand Ministry of Education.

Thouin, M. (1993). L'évaluation des apprentissages en mathématiques : une perspective constructiviste. *Mesure et évaluation en éducation, 16*(1–2), 47–64.

Van de Walle, J.A. (2001). *Elementary and middle school mathematics: Teaching developmentally.* (4th ed.). New York: Addison Wesley Longman.

Wearne, D., & Hiebert, J. (1988). A cognitive approach to meaningful mathematics instruction: Testing a local theory using decimal numbers. *Journal for Research in Mathematics Education, 19*, 371–384.

Wright, R.J., Martland, J., & Stafford, A.K. (2000). *Early numeracy: Assessment for teaching and intervention.* London: Paul Chapman.

Yackel, E. (2001). Perspectives on arithmetic from classroom-based research in the United States of America. In J. Anghileri (Ed.), *Principles in arithmetic teaching: Innovative approaches for the primary classroom* (pp. 15–32). Buckingham, England: Open University Press.